BUILDING A WOOD-FIRED OVEN

FOR

BREAD AND PIZZA

0 10 20 30 40 50 60 70 80 90 100 110 120 130cm

Frontispiece: front elevation of the completed oven (scale 1:20).

BUILDING A WOOD-FIRED OVEN

FOR

BREAD AND PIZZA

TOM JAINE

PROSPECT BOOKS

1996

Published by Prospect Books in 1996,
at Allaleigh House, Blackawton, Totnes, Devon TQ9 7DL.

4th edition reprinted 2000
6th impression 2002
7th impression 2003
9th impresion 2005

A CIP record for this book is available from the British Library.

Typography, design and technical drawings by Tom Jaine.
Cover illustration © 1996, Janet Mills
Illustrations numbered 2,4,5,6,7,9,13,16,17,18,43,48,56,61,62,64,65,68
©1996, Mark Berryman
Illustration of Skipton Castle on page 102, © Peter C.D. Brears
Illustration of Bulgarian oven on page 11, © Maria Kaneva Johnson

ISBN 090732570X

Printed by The Cromwell Press, Trowbridge, Wiltshire.

CONTENTS

Figure 1: a beehive oven, here dep-icted on a wooden stand, housed in a barnlike structure to give shelter. In the foreground, a trough where the dough is kneaded and left to rise.

ACKNOWLEDGEMENTS

I would like to record my debt to many people who have offered advice, help and encouragement to baking at Allaleigh over the past ten years. Ann and Don Barnes, Ed Behr, Roger Berrett, Peter Brears, Alan Davidson, the late Gwenda Hill, Andras Kaldor, Nigel Marriage, Janet Mills, Jim Moore, Polly Morrow, Adam Nicholson, Alan Scott, Brian Stoddart, Rolf Peter Weichold, and Andrew Whitley.

My family have suffered many evenings, and days, of intense tedium. Their patience is impressive.

INTRODUCTORY

Cooking

The list maker can happily tick off ways in which food may be cooked: roasted, grilled, boiled, fried, baked, and .... They all, for that is cooking, require the introduction of heat. And they might, with the addition of smoking – an attenuated form of roasting – be reduced to three: direct exposure to flames or smoke; the use of a heated medium (water or liquid, oil or fat) that transfers that warmth to the food immersed in, or lubricated by it; and finally, cooking in a dry heat at one remove from the flame itself, be it on a griddle or hot stone set atop the fire, or an entire structure (or excavation) that has itself been heated in order to cook the food in the residual heat stored in its walls, floor and ceiling.

Cooking techniques may be viewed as successive steps away from the primitive. At first, direct application of the flame; then the construction of pots to enable heat transference; then the development, over millenniums, of structures to retain heat and return it in measured and useful fashion.

This reflects the broad pattern of development in the food of early man. Roasting is best suited to flesh of all sorts; boiling, or the interposition of a medium, is most apposite for vegetables or fruit, if they are not eaten raw; and baking, on a bakestone or in an oven, is the preferred – though by no means the first – way of coping with grains. Cereals and the settled agriculture they imply came relatively late in man's history – just like ovens.

While a close link between methods of cooking and basic ingredients would be difficult to sustain in every instance – boiling could be applied as well to meat as to vegetables, gruels or fruit – it does become relevant in thinking about wood-fired ovens. We usually refer to them, and they invariably seem to have a primary use, as bread ovens. What was there about bread, therefore, that urged mankind towards ovens?

Bread, and ovens, are essentials of a Mediterranean, near-eastern, and southern European culture. The two are indissoluble, and have colonised the world as supercargoes on the packet-boat of European migration. Where a technique of baking food existed beyond European confines, it was in the form of a pit of heated stones, such as the North American clambake, or the Polynesian paupau: nothing to do with bread, but cooking out of the circulating air, by means of borrowed, indirect, or residual heat.

Bakestones and pot ovens

There are many strategies available for dealing with grain. The technical steps that ended with grinding into flour do not inevitably lead to the beehive oven. At first the seeds may be cracked and made into porridge or gruel. Or the milled flour can be made into a paste and boiled, as with central Asian pasta, or dumplings. Or the paste can be wrapped round sticks and roasted for the Boy Scout favourite, damper. The use of controlled dry heat by means of a flat bakestone or metal griddle, or the surface of the hearthstone itself, once swept of ash and embers, was a further primitive method that appealed to cultures across the world whether in Ethiopia, Pakistan, the Middle East, Latin America, or Brittany and other Celtic upland zones of northern Europe.

The two essential techniques, bakestone and ashes of the hearth, might co-exist. When two Anglo-Saxon historians described Alfred's bloomer with the cakes (which were flatbreads) one described them as burning in the fire, the other has him with a pan and the fire underneath.

Flatbreads, like pancakes, have little or no leavening. They are satisfactorily cooked on a griddle, not requiring the all-round heat of the oven. Griddle baking is not wholly restricted to unleavened breads, even if the 'loaves' are always flat. The Ethiopian *injera*, made from the indigenous grass seed *tef*, was given a sour, natural leavening which makes the giant flatbread much lighter, softer and more spongy than it would otherwise have been. The yeast-raised crumpet or pikelet is also full of holes and spongy in texture. But cooking these on a griddle has inevitable consequences on their form. If a dough is leavened and worked into a shape that requires more complex and gradual application of heat than a griddle can supply, then practical modification is essential.

A bakestone is not the most adaptable of instruments. Its heat is delivered from one side only; whatever is cooked on it will usually have to be turned. But a stone with a cover was a radical improvement, for embers heaped around the lid could provide top heat. In short, an oven, albeit with inadequate temperature control (though Seneca refers to holes in the lids of Roman pot ovens to control the temperature more sensitively). Such a device served to bake soda bread on the peat fires of Ireland, barley bread in Cornwall, or spelt and wheaten breads in south-eastern Europe and the Mediterranean.

These pot ovens have a long recorded history, in classical cultures as well as the barbarian fringes. There were two terms in Latin: *testum* and *clibanus* (from the Greek *klibanos* and ultimately perhaps from the Indo-European root **kleibh-* which may mean 'to bake'), both describing the same vessel designed for cooking between two heats. These figure in later periods as *testo*, *tegamo*, *tiella* and *tian* in various Mediterranean languages, or as the 'trap' in northern France and England. Latin literary references like the instruction by Cato to knead, mould and bake your bread under the *testu*, or pseudo-Virgil's description in *Moretum* of cleaning the hearthstone for the bread, then covering it with tiles before heaping on embers, or Seneca's account of the development of ovens subsequent to the more primitive system of baking in a hot earthenware vessel, confirm the linguistic and archaeological evidence. In the Middle Ages, the technique was often associated with making pies topped with a pastry crust, though the thirteenth-century Bolognese writer Pietro di Crescenzi said that 'bread baked in an oven is better, because it cooks evenly; that cooked in *testi* is not as good', so even in medieval Italy the oven did not reign entirely supreme.

The pot oven lives on in the Balkans, where Maria Kaneva-Johnson describes the *vrshnik* (Macedonian), or portable lidded oven; or on the Dalmatian island of Iz, where the pot goes by the name of *cripnja* (from *clibanus*), while in Romania the word is *test* – a straight-line derivation from the Latin, before the intrusion of the Greek loan-word.

Nor had the tradition entirely disappeared in Cornwall when the Women's Institute compiled their first local cookery book in 1929. A correspondent described arrangements current in the household of her youth where the clay oven was only used once weekly, and the flat iron griddle for every day. The griddle was placed on a trivet over the fire of brambles, furze and sticks which was allowed to burn hot then, as it died to embers, the trivet would be removed and the bakestone placed directly on the hot ashes. Once wiped clean, the bread would be placed on the griddle, a heavy 'baker' – 'like a huge iron frying pan without the handle' – would go over the top, embers would be piled right over and the loaf would take about an hour to cook.

The eighteenth-century writer William Ellis eloquently described this process in an account of baking barley bread in Devonshire,

...under a large iron kettle, that is chiefly made use of for washing dishes in. As soon as the dough is ready, they make it into a loaf of about three parts the size of the kettle; a large kettle will cover a loaf of near half a bushel of flower [approximately 28 lb (12.6 kg), yielding a loaf of approximately 35 lb (15.75 kg)], which being clean and dry, they sweep the hearth, and on the hottest part of it they lay down the loaf, and immediately cover it with the kettle, then put over it a good quantity of damp straw or horse litter, and upon this a few ashes: This done, they set fire to the straw, which will burn leisurely away, and cause the upper part of the loaf to be baked equal to the under part; and to this end they commonly allow four or five hours for baking it, if it is a loaf of moderate size; but if very large, they frequently bake it thus all night.

From pot ovens to brick ovens

To speculate on the century by century progress of leavened bread and its means of cooking would be too much for this place, but the short answer has to be that the covered griddle buried in embers may answer requirements to a degree, but soon becomes practically inadequate for large-scale use, and in a culture where sun-dried bricks and clay are readily available, some larger version of the *clibanus* must have presented itself as a viable alternative. The presumption must surely be that the bakestone and pot oven antedate the beehive oven, even if latterly their courses have run parallel.

The consensus that leavened bread was a discovery of the ancient Egyptians may or may not be confirmed by the fact that the earliest ovens are found in the eastern half of the Mediterranean basin. Excavations in distinct culture zones have produced variant forms, all with us today. An ancient Egyptian oven from the 2nd millennium BC, 'was a squat, beehive-shaped clay mound about three feet tall with internal shelving and with a hole at the base designed to allow the removal of ash. It was principally used to bake bread, although food could also be cooked in a saucepan placed on the flat oven-top, and the cook sat or squatted in front of the mouth of the oven while preparing her food.' From the Jordanian site of Deir' Alla comes a version of the modern tandoor, the *tannur*, dating from around 1000 BC, with a fireplace

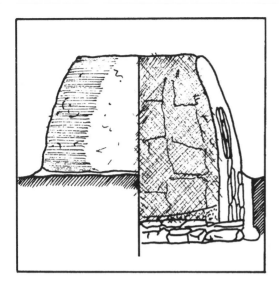

Figure 2: a section and reconstruction of an Iron Age tannur *from Tell Keisan near Deir' Alla in Jordan. The drawing is based on that published by Eveline J. van der Steen.*

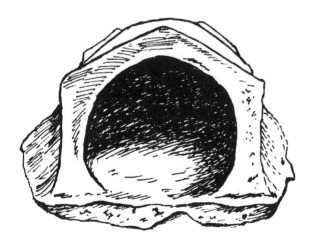

Figure 3: a clay model, dated approximately 4,300 BC, of a bread oven, found in Stara Zagora, Bulgaria; and another of a loaf, carbon-dated to approximately 5,100 BC.

in the bottom of the oven, and a large opening at the top. Pots could also be placed over the aperture, as in Egypt, for cooking as if on an open fire (Figure 2). At Deir' Alla, there was also the *wagdiah*, a closed domed oven or beehive, with two levels. In this case, the fire was built at the bottom, and the bread cooked on the heated floor. This form is sometimes termed, by writers at the beginning of this century for instance, the 'Jewish' oven. Both the *tannur* and *wagdiah* are found in Middle Eastern villages today.

Older than these, however, are the clay models of beehive ovens found in tombs around Stara Zagora in Bulgaria, dating from approximately 4,300 BC, together with models of the loaves baked in them (Figure 3). The pricks in the surface, and the entire shape and appearance of the loaf illustrated must indicate leavening, which would antedate the risen loaves illustrated in Egyptian wall paintings, or those excavated in Egyptian sites. On Minoan Crete, a community that shared the same Mesopotamian-Egyptian cultural nexus as the Nile valley, such ovens do not occur in the archaeological record for another thousand years, so these Bulgarian remains seem to imply a development of bread and baking that was without and beyond the accepted 'cradle of civilisation'.

The Bulgarian finds are the clearest sign of the symbiosis of risen bread and ovens. A paste of flour and water was given a leavening, be it a lactic fermentation from the souring and working together of the two ingredients, or alcoholic fermentation caused by the introduction of yeasts, or a combination of the two, which meant that bubbles of air or expanding gas were created at the very heart of the dough. If the flour was of the right sort, this gas could be trapped within the dough by the cells expanding elastically – the magic of gluten – and it was the operation of the gas which the oven captured and sealed within a crust of sugary starch formed by exposure to heat. No instrument could do this more effectively than an oven.

The Bulgarian oven may be compared to a modern beehive oven from Peru (Figure 4) – the consequence of Spanish invasion and colonisation, not native Inca ingenuity. That there is little to tell them apart speaks volumes for the enduring simplicity and satisfaction of the original concept.

How then does an oven of this nature work? A space is enclosed by floor, walls and roof, with a single aperture at the front. On the floor, or the sole, a fire is kindled. Air enters through the opening to feed the flames, smoke leaves through the same hole, an invisible line separating the incoming and outgoing, bottom and top respectively. The fire heats the entire structure, more or less

Figure 4: a beehive oven made of clay in the courtyard of a house in Peru. Drawing based on a photograph in The Cook's Room. *The ledge on the left is a working platform, the stone door is propped up in the front.*

Figure 5: a drawing based on a photograph of a modern tannur oven maker's shop in Turkey.

efficiently depending on its size and shape, and the competence of the fire-builder and the fuel used. At a certain moment, the structure is deemed sufficiently hot for the purpose of baking and the fire and ashes are withdrawn. In their place is thrust the risen dough. The aperture is closed and the loaf cooks in the residual heat which will, if the architecture is sound, radiate in equal amount from all angles thus browning the loaf evenly and allowing the action of leavening to take effect in all parts of the dough. On the elapse of time gauged by experience, the door is opened, the loaf removed and left to cool.

There may be an infinity of variables, caused by design, weather, materials, skill, location and mere happenstance, but that is how all bread ovens worked until modern times. The fuel can be anything, provided it burns; the heat may be delivered by a variety of routes; the oven can be made of many different materials, in a whole range of shapes and sizes, but the principle of residual, radiant heat is enduring. The bread oven differs from the normal run of domestic appliances because the heat combines radiation from the structure itself, and the convection heat of the air contained within the cooking space. Many domestic ovens rely on convection alone, which gives a different character to the bread cooked in them, particularly to the crust.

While the oven was developed to cook bread, its utility was more general. It was bread first and last because loaves are not amenable to other forms of cookery in quite the same way as a gigot of lamb that could as easily be roasted or broiled. And it was bread first because it occupies a rather more important place in the hierarchy of foodstuffs than fruit cake, sponges or meringues. But they too need an oven, were always cooked in the bread oven, and still can be. Similarly, stews and casseroles may take their place on the sole, and joints of meat or pies that are to be baked. Samuel Pepys's venison pasties were never cooked at home, but at the baker or the cookshop; so too were countless Sunday joints, whose consumers boasted too meagre a fire to undertake a full-scale roast.

In Cornwall, again, a news story of 1948 recounts how the housewives of the fishing port of Mousehole lacked the necessary to bake their Christmas cakes: they themselves did not have adequate ranges or stoves, and the last public baker of the town had retired. 'Many women were to be seen carrying large baskets along the cliff path or to the bus on the way to Newlyn, where ovens had to serve scores of extra patrons.' Such practices might be observed anywhere in Europe.

Oven basics

Ovens are simple structures. Figure 6 is a cut-away of a clay oven in Quebec, common since the eighteenth century, and the subject of a revealing monograph published by the National Museum in Canada. A superstructure of alder withies is woven together on a rough boulder foundation floored with stiff clay, and then plastered with tempered clay. An iron door is built into the structure. The clay dries slowly in the sunshine and the wooden supports are burned out during the first firing. There is normally an over-arching roof that shelters the oven, and sometimes the workers, from the rigours of weather. These are outdoor ovens and they rarely had chimneys or flues.

These Quebec ovens were graphically described in the eighteenth century:

> At a small distance from the house make a platform, of
> about six or seven feet square, of earth, stone, or wood,
> raise it about three feet from the ground, procure a quantity
> of clay, and one third sand, beat and mix them well with
> water to the consistence of brick earth; with this clay cover
> the top of the square, about six or seven inches thick, and
> level it properly.

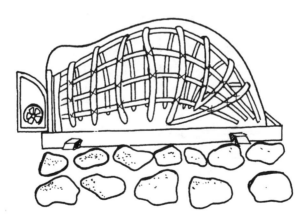

Figure 6: a view of a Quebec oven, showing the boulder foundation, the withy or lath framwork on which the clay envelope is formed, and the iron doors in place.

Then provide a number of laths, twigs, or small branches of trees, that will easily bend in an oval shape, and on the moist clay mark out the size of the oven, leaving at one end a vacancy for the door, in proportion to the size, sticking the ends of them into the clay. When finished it will appear like a basket overset. Then begin and plaster it over with clay, about an inch at a time, and when it has dried a little, lay on more, until it is about eight or nine inches thick, when finished, and dry, fill the oven with wood or coals, and set it on fire, and wherever any cracks are seen in the arch, pour in some clay and plaister it over. The fire must be continued till the whole is burnt to a brick. (From A. Edlin, *A Treatise on the Art of Bread-Making*, 1805, quoting Captain Cochrane, *Seaman's Guide*.)

The shape of the oven here illustrated is ovoid, with a domed roof. It answers well the demands of the materials used. But the more common shape, especially among early ovens, is an approximate hemisphere. This is seen in figure 7, or in the oven in Peru illustrated above.

Figure 7: an outdoor oven, from a fifteenth-century French manuscript. The loaves are characteristically round – at least when represented in pictures. There are trestles of loaves proving and the lady is charging the oven with the aid of a peel.

The movement of air in ovens of this character is simply illustrated in figure 8. It enters through the front aperture at the bottom, and leaves through the same opening, at the top. The smoke may be simply voided into the atmosphere at that point, or may be guided up a flue. The oven pictured in figure 9 has a cowl over the door, which vents through the roof to the sky above. It is a medieval baker's shop, the man in the process of discharging the loaves to the vendeuse with her basket. By way of contrast, the busy bakery in figure 10, with two ovens hard at work, bread in the foreground and pies beyond, has no flues, the smoke doubtless wafting around to everyone's discomfort. Precisely that arrangement was in force in the medieval kitchen at Stanton Harcourt, in Oxfordshire (Figures 11 and 12). Only the height of the cathedral-like room (compare the abbatial kitchens at Glastonbury or Fontevraud) ensured some clean air to the workers, although testimony from Roman emperors to chefs like Carême is proof enough of the enervating effect of smoke and fumes.

These hemispheres can be grasped in the sections and plans of an oven by Alan Scott, the Californian oven-crafter (Figure 13), where he has embedded a preformed terracotta oven in an insulating envelope of brick and concrete.

There are various factors that will affect performance. The size of the front aperture determines the amount of oxygen feeding the fire. If it is small, in relation to the height of the vault inside, then the fire will burn slowly, sometimes frustratingly so – recall that at least half the aperture will be occupied by fumes on the way out, not in. The ideal is that the front opening should be at least 63 per cent of the overall height of the internal space.

The shape of the oven's interior will affect how evenly it heats, and how it returns that heat to the loaves once placed on the oven sole. A circle is geometrically sound. It is not, however, essential. The oven that is the model for

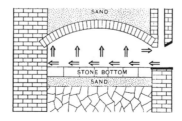

Figure 8: airflow in a traditional oven.

Figure 9: a fifteenth-century French manuscript illustration of a town bakery (from Tacuinum Sanitatis, *the same source as figure 7). The oven has a cowl over the door, and a chimney on the roof above.*

Figure 10: a drawing based on a fifteenth-century French woodcut of a bakery with bread being prepared in the foreground, pies in the second oven behind. A boy is moulding rolls next to the baker. Faggot and cord wood is at the ready. The working surface close to the oven is reminiscent of that in figure 4.

Figure 11: the medieval kitchen at Stanton Harcourt, Oxfordshire. A nineteenth-century view, but the building survives. The cook is shown at a dough trough, kneading on the cover. Faggot wood is stored to one side. A peel leans against the trough. The smoke vents through the louvres of the roof above.

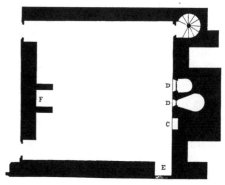

Figure 12: a plan of the kitchen at Stanton Harcourt. The cupboard at C was perhaps an aumbry used to store the leaven dough from one baking day to the next.

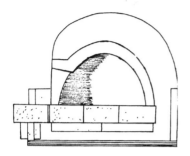

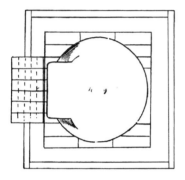

Figure 13: plan and elevation based on proposals by Alan Scott, the Californian oven-crafter, showing a preformed terracotta oven shell embedded in a concrete envelope with a brick baking sole and threshold.

the building project that is this book is based on a square or rectangle, and yet gives off its heat evenly enough. Ceilings are usually vaulted because that form is self-supporting. Flat-roofed, or ripple-roofed ovens have been built, using iron girders as supports, but their interruption of the smooth surface can cause cool spots from uneven airflow, and the fire may affect the integrity of the metal beams. Modern ovens for commercial use are often flat-roofed.

Finally, the oven is not only the shape of its interior and the size of its door, it is also the insulating structure wrapped around it. Figure 14 is an advertisement for a late nineteenth-century American oven and shows to an extreme the relationship between insulation and the baking chamber – reached by the small central door. The fire is maintained in the boiler at the bottom right, and hot air circulated through the structure by means of several flues. If insulation is insufficient, all the heat created by the fire will simply waste away. Plans for a useful oven have to allow enough space for ample insulation.

While many ovens are vented through their doors, more careful attention to flues and chimneys can alter or improve the performance. Similarly, a great leap forward in oven design was made when the fire was made more

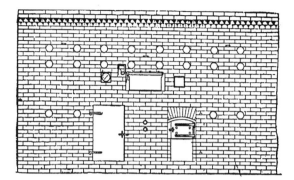

Figure 14: an advertisement of c. 1891 for an American commercial bread oven.

independent of the cooking space itself, for instance in the side-fired Scotch oven which became current in parts of Britain during the nineteenth century.

Figure 15 shows the plan of such a design. The fireplace is fuelled and ventilated by a separate door, and the flue is put in the opposite corner to permit the spread of heat. Not only can the fire be maintained ready for reheating the oven in a long baking session, but these arrangements allow the fire to burn more fiercely. It is suitable for the larger ovens that were needed for large urban bakeries.

The author A. Edlin was writing about bread at just the time that oven technology was changing. His account of bakehouse arrangements at the beginning of the nineteenth century is instructive.

A Bakehouse is a manufactory where bread is made for the purposes of sale. In order to render it convenient, it should be attached to the dwelling house, and have an inner door opening into the kitchen, and likewise an outer door to

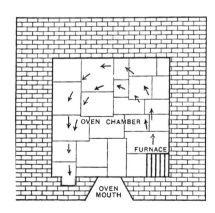

Figure 15: airflow diagram of a Scotch oven.

open into a small yard. In this yard there ought to be a well or pump, as also a shed for the piling of faggots. The room should be large and commodious, and the floor laid with stone or tiles. On one side should be erected a dresser or counter, with suitable shelves above it; on another side a kneading trough, about seven feet long, three feet high, two feet and a half broad at top, and sixteen inches at bottom, with a sluice board to pen the dough up at one end, and a lid to shut down like that of a box. On the third side a copper that will contain from three to four pails of water should be erected, which is far preferable to the filthy custom of heating the water in the oven; and on the fourth side the oven should be placed. A bakehouse built upon this plan will, perhaps, be as commodious as art can render it; but, of late years, an alteration has been made in the manner of fitting up the oven and copper, that both may be heated with the same fire.

In order to comprehend the usefulness of this improvement, it will be necessary to state that an oven, built upon the old principle, is usually of an oval shape; the sides and bottom of brick, tiles, and lime, and arched over at top with a door in front; and, at the upper part, an enclosed closet with an iron grating, for the tins to stand on, called the proving oven. To heat these ovens the faggots are introduced and burnt to an ash; it is then removed, and the bottom cleaned out. This takes up a considerable space of time, during which period a great deal of heat escapes. A still farther length of time is necessary for putting in the bread, and unless much more fuel is expended than is really necessary, in heating an oven upon this principle, it gets chilled before the loaves are all set in, and the bread is, therefore, liable to fall; a circumstance that unavoidably renders it heavy.

To remedy this inconvenience, many intelligent bakers have, within these few years past, had their ovens built upon a solid base of brick and lime, with a door of iron furnished with a damper to carry off the steam as it rises.

On one side of it is placed a fire-place with a grating, ash-hole, and iron door, similar to that under a copper, with a partition to separate it from the oven, and open at the end. Over this is erected a middling-sized copper with a cock at the bottom, and on one side of it is placed the proving oven; the whole being faced with brick and plaister.

The distinction between domestic, stove and commercial ovens is well expressed in the Houlston's Industrial Library volume *The Baker*, a small manual of instruction produced at the turn of this century.

A good oven is necessary for the production of good bread. If the oven be heated, as in country places, by dry wood, furze, or fern, burnt in the oven itself, it ought to be built round, not long, as there will be in the former case a greater equality of heat. The roof should be from twenty inches to two feet high in the centre; the mouth no larger than will be sufficient to admit the bread. But many people who make their own bread send it to be baked at the baker's. We have seen good ovens attached to a stove, and heated by the kitchen fire. These are not sufficiently capacious to contain loaves enough for the consumption of a large family, but they answer the purpose of a small family very well. To save room, it will be necessary, in stove ovens, to bake in tins. Bread thus baked is much more smooth and neat than when baked in the ordinary way; but the pleasant crispness of the crust is wanting.

The ovens used in London and some other large towns are, for the most part, heated by a furnace placed on one side. The heat in these ovens is very equable, and the baker is enabled to keep it up at all times with very little trouble, and with less expense than by the old method.

There were more ad hoc devices for concentrating draught, such as the coal cradle and blowpipe in figure 16, which serve as reminder that not every oven burned wood. Coal ovens were heated by moving the grate around, and though most wood-fired ovens burned their fuel straightforwardly from front

Figure 16: coal cradle and blowpipe from a nineteenth-century British oven.

to back, it was possible to vary the pattern of combustion to ensure that heat got to every part. Peat-fired ovens, for example, were often started off with the fire ranged down one side – perhaps to give a greater surface area on which the oxygen could play.

The larger the oven, the more complicated the flue arrangement. Inside big medieval ovens, you will often find an extra vent tucked to one side or at the back – an example is the oven in the fortress of Castelnaud in the Dordogne. This allowed for a through draught during the firing, and could be closed by a damper once heat had been achieved.

The Hertfordshire author William Ellis of Little Gaddesden wrote *The Country Housewife's Companion* in 1750, with infinite detail about cookery and country practices, in which he discusses just such a supplementary flue.

> Mr. Mortimer says, it may not be improper for the baking of bread to insert an oven, which a friend of mine (says he) has made, at the further end of which he has made a vent for the smoak, which, if he had carried upright, would have obliged him to have been at the charge [cost] of a particular funnel [flue and chimney pot] for it; besides he could not have well come at it, to stop it up when the oven was hot, and therefore he brought it with a pipe over the top of the oven, by which means he can stop both the mouth and vent together. He tells me, that the air drawing through the oven, his wood kindles presently, and that any green wood will burn in it. He says, it takes up but one third part of the wood, that another sort of oven takes up to heat it; also that brick ovens heat much sooner and better than those made with stone.

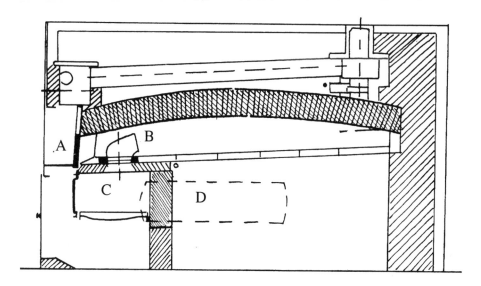

Figure 17: a section of a gueulard *ove. A is the oven door, sliding upwards to open; B is the* gueule; *C is the firebox; D is the hot water tank.*

An interconnected flue of this sort is in fact to be seen in the *gueulard* in figure 17. As in the Scotch oven in figure 15, the internal flue may still be at the front of the oven space, but its very existence means that the oven door can be lower, as it does not have to fulfil the two functions of inhalation and exhaustion. This can be important if you wish to preserve the internal atmosphere of the oven during multiple baking, for a low door will trap the superheated air containing the evaporated moisture from cooked loaves.

The fire is in a furnace placed below the mouth of the oven and the heat directed into the oven chamber by means of a large pipe (*gueule* = mouth). The fire also serves to heat water, contained in the tank marked by a broken line in the drawing. The roof is arched, and the floor slopes up towards the back of the oven space, where there is also a flue controlled by a damper. The purpose of this sloping floor was to create a volume of air above the level of the top of the door so that steam and superheated vapour released by the action of baking bread would not escape as soon as the door was opened. Moisture has a great effect on the crunch and bloom of the crust, as well as allowing a few precious extra moments of expansion to the dough in the first blast of heat. This was well expressed by Herman Senn in his edition of Mrs Beeton's *Household Management* (quoted by Elizabeth David):

The unsuitability of the modern oven [he means a domestic oven in a cooking range] is principally due to thinness of the sides and the fact that it is not airtight; consequently all the steam escapes, rendering the bread dry and the crust hard and chippy, and not moist and crisp like baker's bread or bread baked in a large brick-built oven. For it should be remembered that it is absolutely necessary to keep all the steam in the oven when baking bread, for the vapour assists the crust to assume the brightness and gloss seen on new bread, known as 'bloom'.

The sloping floor was an innovation of the later eighteenth century, when Viennese techniques were transplanted to France, which began to excel in the *viennoiserie* which produced the *baguettes*, *bâtards* and *ficelles* with which we are now familiar. The arrangement was used in combination with quite complex devices for dispensing water drip by drip at the back of the oven to increase the amount of steam in the atmosphere. In modern ovens, steam is available at the touch of a button, but for our purposes, extra steam is technical overkill, though a slightly sloping floor may have other advantages. So long as the oven chamber is kept well-sealed, and a good swoosh with the scuffle is given shortly before charging, conditions should be adequate to produce a handsome loaf of bread.

CONSTRUCTION

The oven design which is outlined in this book is a free-standing structure, with approximate dimensions of 2 metres square on the ground by 2.5 metres to the base of the chimney pot. It is simple to build: for a novice block- and brick-layer. Hence, for example, although the brick roof is arched, it is not domed. The book is equipped with measured drawings developed with the tyro in mind. Plans and elevations detail each block and brick that needs to be laid to achieve the desired end. Nothing, I hope, is left to the imagination, except finishing touches: the roof, the surface render or finish to the outside walls. If you get thus far, you will by then be adept enough to finish the job under your own steam. In a later chapter I suggest alternative architectural treatments you may wish to explore. None of these affects the working of the oven itself, merely how much you enjoy its presence in your garden.

Preliminaries

Before embarking on the project, you need to have the right materials, the correct equipment, the proper site, and have satisfied the various legal authorities that may have higher powers over land irreducibly yours.

The regulations

To take the last first. Whether you require permissions from local authorities for planning, smoke control or building regulation purposes will depend on the status of the territory you occupy. Because these matters vary from place to place, I venture no specific advice. However, I stress the need to satisfy their demands before commencing work. Their wrath, if spurned, can be vengeful; and will certainly be a nuisance.

People in urban areas with smoke controls, or people who live in historic areas protected by legislation against new developments, will have more to contend with than those who build their oven in isolation, with few neighbours and complaisant (to a degree) local guardians. A small structure, *if it is not in sight of a public highway*, will not require planning permission, whether free-standing, or attached to the house or other buildings. It will fall under the category of 'permitted development', as one is allowed to add a certain percentage to the existing area of a dwelling. Building regulations, which cover structures for habitable purposes, or with connections to drainage services, do not apply.

The site

The site of the oven needs careful thought. The design given in this book is free-standing, but of course many ovens, yesterday and today, are within, part of or attached to buildings. This may raise questions of fire-proofing, fire prevention, smoke and emission control that are complex and delicate. Which is why I have avoided them to a large extent. Some discussion of ovens attached to existing houses is included in the chapter about oven restoration, below. An observation, to steady or quell the vapours of ambition, is that the great fire of London was started by a spark from a baker's oven. Free-standing ovens are less convenient on days of rain and tempest, but my presumption has been that the reader is a fair-weather baker. In Quebec and Switzerland,

Figure 18: a summer kitchen in the Balkans, with a roof to protect against the rain. The oven has an internal flue, the damper can be seen above the door. The flat top is here a useful storage shelf.

for example, where communal free-standing ovens survive, they have overarching roofs to protect against the elements (or see the oven in figure 18). Some such arrangement can be easily achieved.

The oven needs to be on a level foundation. It is easier, therefore, if the ground is level in the first place, and advantageous the ground be firm. Should there be doubts about its stability, were it very sandy or a light clay with a soft subsoil, the foundations may need to be deeper than specified.

It is helpful if the site is not too exposed to the wind. If the oven mouth is placed out of the prevailing wind, the best compromise will be achieved. Given there is much smoke during the early part of firing, family and neighbours will be none too pleased with a constant stream through their open windows. Appreciation of the prevailing wind is all that is needed. The amount of smoke will vary according to materials burned and the speed of ignition (in turn affected by the level of draught). Be consoled that smoke is light once a strong flame is burning and the fuel has turned to charcoals and embers.

Remember that foundations are below ground. Check, therefore, they will not damage or invade any subterranean services such as drains, water pipes, or electrical or telephone conduits.

The most important factor in choosing your site will be the relationship between the oven and any existing buildings. On windy nights, there will often be sparks flying when you come to rake out the embers, no matter how carefully. The oven should be so placed that these do not constitute a danger. If it is too close to buildings, it may suffer from poor draught or from those violent tornado effects that are felt when walking through a forest of high-rise buildings. The chief disadvantage of having the oven too far from the building itself is that the bread, pizza or whatever will be prepared in the kitchen and have to be carried to and from the place of cooking. The shorter the distance, particularly on stormy nights, the better.

For my own part, the oven is 8 metres from the house, downwind, and capable of illumination from an external floodlight. This is just about the maximum distance for rushing to and fro when rain threatens. It is constructed on the edge of a spread of hard-standing so there is no danger of slipping on mud or debris as I carry a load of proved loaves delicately towards the work-station before charging the oven.

The equipment

The oven is low-tech building. Without extending the instructions into a discourse on elementary bricklaying, the following items of equipment are probably essential to complete the work with dispatch. All may be purchased at the builders' merchant.

A tape measure
A cement mixer (optional)
A shovel
A pick axe
A wheelbarrow
A bucket
A stiff broom
A mason's trowel
A lump hammer
A bolster
A spirit level (for level and plumb)
Hacksaw
Various tools for carpentry (for making the roof – optional)

Materials

The materials for this oven are basic indeed. The quantities I have suggested are approximate. I have not listed all the little things that will crop up in the course of construction, presuming your backyard, or the rubbish tip, can provide many incidentals.

Builders' sand, 3 tons
Combined aggregate for concrete, 2 tons
Hydrated lime, 3 x 50 kg bags
Portland cement, 3 x 50 kg bags
Common bricks, 225 x 75 x 112.5mm (nominal), approximately 160
Fire bricks, 220 x 75 x 105mm, approximately 160
Engineering bricks, 225 x 60 x 112.5mm (nominal), approximately 250
Concrete blocks, 450 x 225 x 100mm (nominal), approximately 160
Concrete lintels, 110 x 65mm (nominal), 2 x 1 metre long
Concrete lintels, 110 x 65mm (nominal), 3 x 2 metres long

Damp-proof course, 10 metres x 150mm
Concrete paving slabs, 2, each measuring 425mm square
BRC fabric reinforcing mesh, 1 sheet of 3.6 x 2.2 metres, 10mm gauge,
   approximately 4 square metres
Plastic damp-proof membrane, approximately 4 square metres

Where the block and brick sizes are noted as nominal, allowance has been made for 10mm of mortar between the joints.

Before buying any finishing materials, as may be used for the oven door, the roof, and the chimney pot, the approximate cost, at 1996 prices, is £500. This may be considerably reduced by using secondhand materials, particularly the bricks and, though sometimes more difficult to find, the concrete blocks.

The mortar and concrete

Because the structure is subject to heat, hence expansion and contraction, a fairly weak lime mortar is proposed for all the brick and block work. This should be made of one part (by volume) Portland cement, one part hydrated lime and six parts sand. If the lime and sand are mixed together with enough water to make a stiff paste, it can be stored, covered, for many weeks. On the day that work begins, add the Portland cement and more water to make a usable mortar. Do not mix too much mortar in advance. This mortar can be used for all the brick and block work.

The concrete may be mixed with one part (by volume) cement, one part hydrated lime, 5 parts combined or all-in aggregate, and water.

The foundations

Mark out a shape on the ground as given in figure 19 using pegs and string. This is 150mm larger than the dimensions of the oven structure. The shape is that of a large square (the oven) and a smaller rectangular 'nose' stuck on the front of it – which is the ash pit and working surface set before the oven mouth. If you are anxious about making right angles, construct a builder's square to test them. Dig down to a depth of 350mm across the whole foundation and remove the spoil to a safe place. It will be reused later.

If the soil is friable, retain the excavation with boards so the sides do not collapse inwards. Otherwise, ensure they are cleanly dressed and vertical.

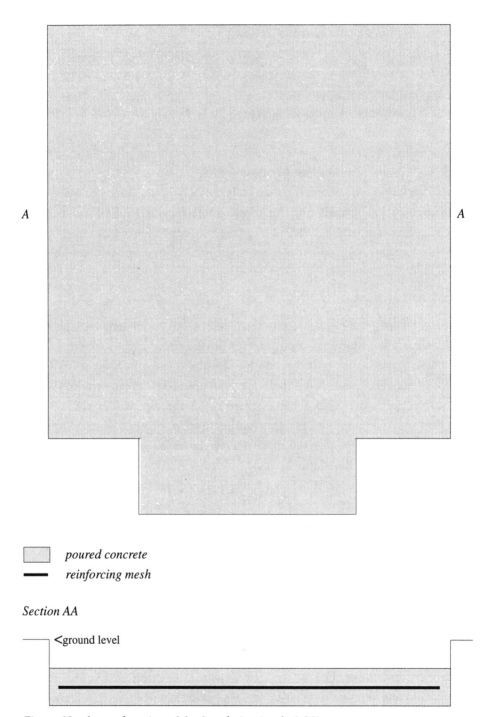

poured concrete

reinforcing mesh

Section AA

<ground level

Figure 19: plan and section of the foundation (scale 1:20).

0 10 20 30 40 50 60 70 80 90 100 110 120 130cm

Line the hole with builders' blue plastic sheeting as a damp-proof membrane. Mix the concrete and pour enough to fill to a depth of 100mm. Place a square of reinforcing mesh, cut from the larger rectangle that has been bought for the job as a whole, over the area that will be beneath the oven itself – you do not have to worry about the area which protrudes in front of the main rectangle. Pour the remainder of the concrete to fill the foundation to a level of 200mm in total. Strike it level.

To ensure that the foundation is poured to a uniform level, insert pegs in the ground just outside the damp-proof membrane (this should not be pierced). Use one peg as the datum, and take levels from that.

The surface finish of the foundation should be brushed with a stiff brush rather than polished smooth with a trowel, to give some key for the first course of blocks. Let it cure for a few days before starting work on the rest of the structure.

The beginning of the oven supporting base

Figure 20 shows the plan and section of the first course of blocks. The plan makes apparent that the oven sits on the larger square, with the ash and cinder box protruding in front. The gap between the two central front blocks is so the ash may later be removed by means of a small shovel.

Although there are not many blocks needing to be cut, the inclusion of the ash pit does mean splitting some. They should be cut with the bolster and lump hammer.

After the first course, the damp-proof course is installed. This is marked in the section in figure 20 by a thick black line on top of the blocks.

The second, third and fourth courses

The next three courses of block work complete the construction of the oven base. There is little of moment to notice, save perhaps the detail of the construction of the ash pit. A common brick is used to reduce the need to split blocks. Figures 21, 22 and 23 are plans of each of these courses.

The only important exception to plain-sailing block work is the installation of the concrete lintels, illustrated in figure 23, in the fourth course. The blocks will have to be chopped out to make room for the lintels, which are laid so as to be flush with the top of the blocks.

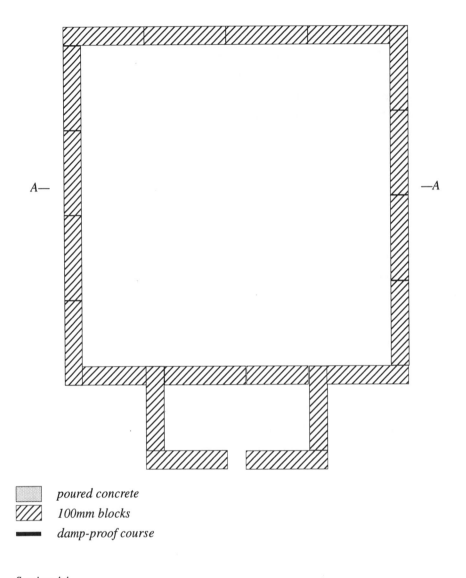

    poured concrete
    100mm blocks
    damp-proof course

Section AA

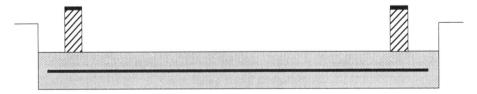

Figure 20: plan and section of the first course of blocks (scale 1:20).

0   10   20   30   40   50   60   70   80   90   100 110 120 130cm

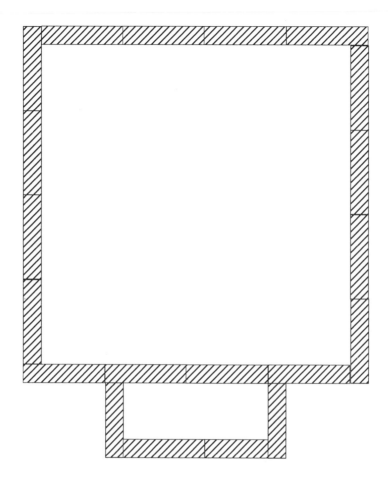

 100mm blocks

Figure 21: plan of the second course of blocks (scale 1:20).

0 10 20 30 40 50 60 70 80 90 100 110 120 130cm

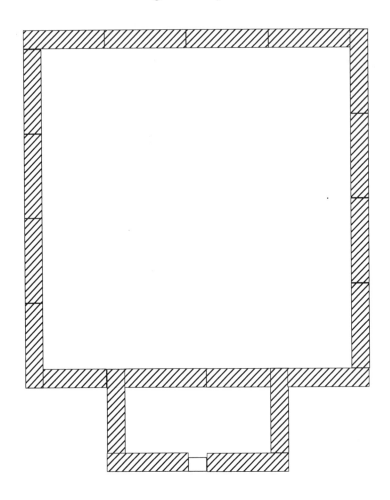

	100mm blocks
	common brick

Figure 22: plan of the third course of blocks (scale 1:20).

0 10 20 30 40 50 60 70 80 90 100 110 120 130cm

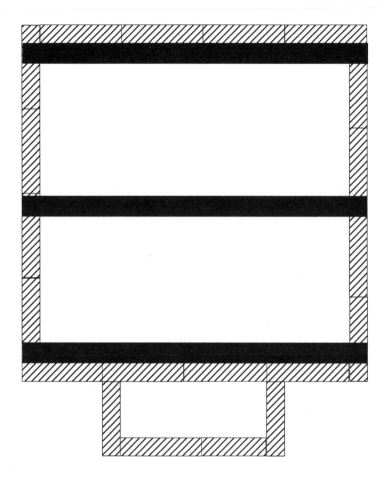

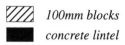 100mm blocks
concrete lintel

Figure 23: plan of the fourth course of blocks (scale 1:20).

0   10   20   30   40   50   60   70   80   90   100 110 120 130cm

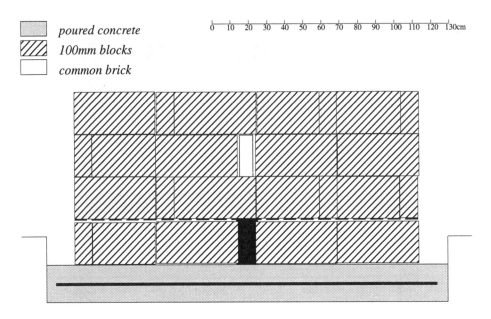

Figure 24: front elevation of the first four courses of blocks (scale 1:20).

When they have been completed, the spoil that was removed during the excavation of the foundation should be backfilled into the void enclosed by the oven's supporting walls – but not into the ash pit. The earth should be tamped down and made level with the top of the blocks and lintels. It will then form a support for casting the concrete slab that takes the oven chamber. If there is insufficient earth, take some from the garden or rubbish heap.

Creating the sole of the oven, and laying the fifth course

All that has gone before is but preparation for the actual oven. The strategy adopted so far is one of solidity. This is by no means the only solution. The solid box might have been hollow, with an open front, supporting a reinforced platform for the oven on its side walls, enabling wood to be stored in the undercroft thus created. This is the arrangement in the eighteenth-century French oven illustrated by figure 53. Such a scheme, however, does not allow for the safe disposal of ashes and cinders, which is a principal reason for the design we have described here. A second advantage of having a solid base is that the under floor insulation (and the outer structure as a whole is only there to provide insulation for the oven within) is better than a void.

The first thing to do is to lay the fifth course of blocks as detailed in the plan in figure 25. Where the mouth of the oven will be, lay 2 courses of engineering bricks (labelled c), rather than blocks. The blocks at right angles (labelled b) are lined up to each side of the ash pit and will support the chimney above.

Before installing this pair of blocks, bed a small strip of iron or steel, running from one side of the ash pit to the other, into the mortar beneath them. It should be about 100mm from the front of the oven. This strip will support one side of a counter top of slate or concrete slabs placed across the top of the ash pit – their other side being supported by the front of the pit itself.

Around the perimeter of the main structure, place strips of polystyrene 10mm thick and at least 110mm tall on the tops of the lintels and the earth backfill. This will serve as an expansion joint for the concrete plate and the mortar poured on top of that.

Pour a 35mm layer of concrete across the area so marked in the plan. Place the BRC reinforcing mesh cut to the size of the slab, less 25mm all round so that the mesh is enclosed entirely by concrete. Complete pouring the concrete to give a level slab, 70mm thick. Allow to set over a day and a night.

Mix a batch of mortar and spread a layer 40mm thick over the concrete slab. Ensure that it is level. Trowel it smooth and leave it to harden for a day or two. Remove the polystyrene that has filled the expansion joint round these two plates or slabs. If it cannot be taken out with a spike or fingers, burn it out with a blow lamp.

Over the entire surface, spread a level layer of sand about 10mm thick. It can spill into the expansion joint, do not worry. Smooth it over carefully. It is easier if it is wetted.

Now comes the laying of the oven floor or sole, using fire bricks laid on edge, without mortar, except for those at the front in the oven mouth. The oven chamber itself is built on top of the sole, although alternative designs often finish the sole independently of the walls. When baking in a commercial oven was continuous, the first thing to need renewal was the sole, worn down by constant raking and dragging of tins, and clumsy or forceful use of the peel. Sometimes, too, the brickwork of the vaulted ceiling would need repointing. These were the most punishing of tasks and had to be done in as small a window of time as possible so the baker would not lose too much revenue from missed firings. The French eighteenth-century author Parmentier has a grand evocation of the undertaking, from dragging the

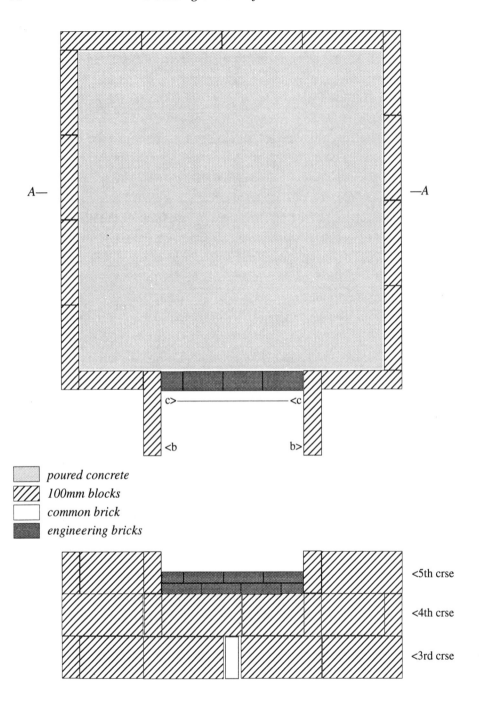

Figure 25: plan of fifth course and supporting slab, with front elevation (scale 1:20).

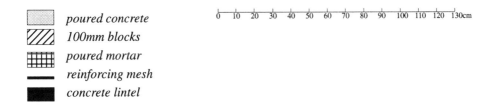

poured concrete
100mm blocks
poured mortar
reinforcing mesh
concrete lintel

0 10 20 30 40 50 60 70 80 90 100 110 120 130cm

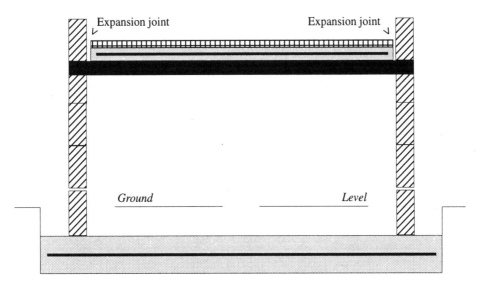

Figure 26: section through AA (figure 25), showing the base slab poured, and the layer of mortar laid above—before the installation of the oven floor.

objecting ovenwright from his bed to watching him work in stifling conditions, prone or supine, repairing the fabric. Although it is possible that the floor of this oven will show some decline in condition over the years, it is unlikely it will need renewal in quite so wholesale a way. In any event, as the fire bricks are not in fact mortared, they can be prised out of position quite easily once access is made by removing the front rank.

A song about the village baker that was once current in the Wiltshire village of Purton also shows the need for constant renewal of the oven fabric. Job Jenkins was loitering in the churchyard when he had the brainwave to use the old tombstones as a new floor for his oven. Quickly coming to an arrangement with the parish clerk, he had the mason install them. To his horror, when he withdrew the first batch of bread baked on the new floor, he found the mason had placed the tombstones inscription uppermost so that instead of a baker's mark, each loaf bore some phrase from the funerary inscription.

> The words on every loaf were marked
> That had on tombstone been,
> One quartern had 'in memory of'
> Another 'here to pine,'
> The third 'departed from this life
> At the age of ninety nine.'

Figure 27 shows the layout of the fire bricks. They do not extend the full width or length of the space enclosed by the perimeter walls, as that would be wasteful. Note that the joints are staggered (save for the front rank), as if they were mortared bricks standing vertically in a wall. Begin by bedding the bricks in the oven mouth in mortar. Joggle them close together. Then lay the oven floor from this given point towards the edges. When you have laid all those shown in the plan, fill the gap between the bricks and the perimeter wall with sand, to ensure that there is no movement of the outside rows of bricks during the next stages.

The first two courses of the oven chamber

The oven itself is constructed from high-fired engineering bricks. These are sufficiently hard to withstand the intense heat, and are cheaper than fire bricks. Fire bricks were used for the sole because they tend to get even hotter, glowing red when the fire has been on them for some hours. The mortar used is the same weak lime mix that has been used throughout. Fire cement, which is expensive, is not necessary.

If the first course is laid as illustrated in figure 29, ensure that the second course is laid so that joints are staggered between the courses. The mortar on the inside of the oven should be tidy. Brush the joints clean after a night has elapsed and the mortar has almost gone off.

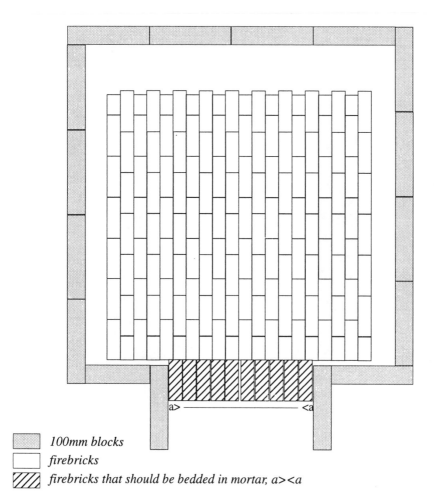

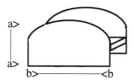
100mm blocks

firebricks

firebricks that should be bedded in mortar, a><a

Figure 27: plan illustrating the laying of the firebrick sole of the oven (scale 1:20).

0 10 20 30 40 50 60 70 80 90 100 110 120 130cm

Figure 28: the former for the oven door arch. The measurement a—a (from the base to the crown of the arch) is 245mm; b—b is 450mm. a—a has been adjusted to allow for 10mm wedges to support the former in position.

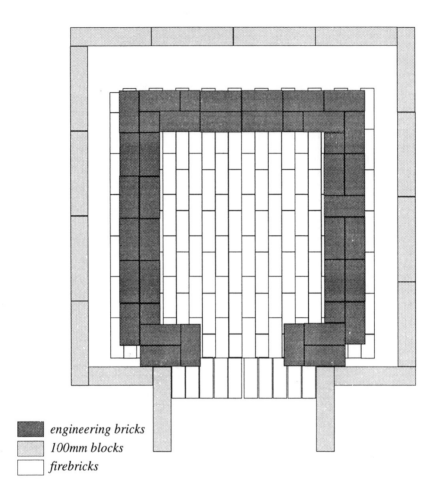

Figure 29: the first course of engineering bricks for the oven chamber (scale 1:20).

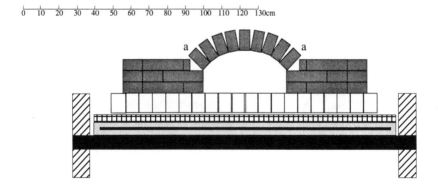

Figure 30: elevation of the front of the oven, showing the arch over the door. The gap between the mortar and the firebricks is occupied by 1cm of sand (scale 1:20).

The third course of the oven chamber and the arch for the doorway

There are two strategies available for forming the oven doorway. Either a brick arch may be turned, or the superstructure of the chimney and flue can be supported on concrete lintels. This plan adopts the first, but concrete lintels will do the job and pose few problems of building technique.

Make two templates of the arch out of heavy plywood such as is used for concrete shuttering. Nail them each side of a piece of 100 x 50mm timber so that the form is free-standing. See figure 28 for approximate dimensions. The vertical measurement is 10mm shorter than the actual height of the arch, so that the former can be placed on wedges of 10mm wood. It will otherwise be difficult to remove once the arch is built, but this way, the wedges have only to be extracted and the form can be pulled free.

Place this form in the doorway. The brick arch is one brick thick, laid lengthwise on edge. The elevation in figure 30 shows how it will look.

Before actually beginning the arch, complete laying the third course of engineering bricks for the oven walls. Once more, stagger the joints. The only differences between second and third courses are the bricks that abut the springing of the door arch. These are labelled (a) in figure 30. Cut them cleanly to size, and bed the first brick of the arch generously in mortar.

Turn the arch over the form work, bedding each brick in mortar. There is no need to shape the bricks into wedges, but the mortar should be well packed.

Turning the oven arch, and laying the fourth course of the oven walls

It will have been appreciated by now that this oven is not a domed beehive oven of traditional form. This is because a barrel arch as specified here is easier to construct, especially with materials readily available from local builders' merchants, than a dome. There may be objections that the rectangular shape of the oven is less rapid to heat, and that the heat radiation is less even, but I have not found this matters in practice, particularly if the firing is fairly long and slow.

Begin by laying the fourth course of bricks along each side of the oven. These are part bricks, approximately 140mm long. They are shown in figure 31, as is the way they should be laid.

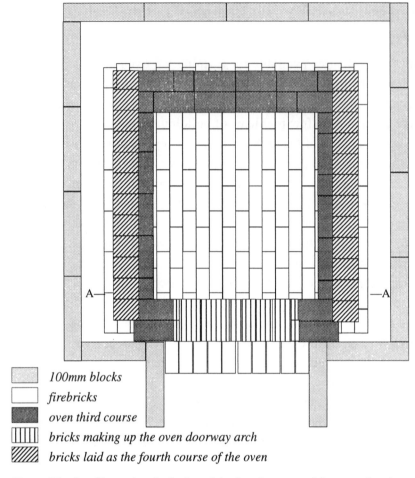

100mm blocks

firebricks

oven third course

bricks making up the oven doorway arch

bricks laid as the fourth course of the oven

Figure 31: plan illustrating the laying of the fourth course of the oven chamber, and showing the arch to the oven door in place (scale 1:20).

0   10   20   30   40   50   60   70   80   90   100   110   120   130cm

Figure 32: elevation of the front of the oven, showing the fourth course of bricks in place, ready to receive the arch of the oven roof (scale 1:20)

The roof arch laps over that of the doorway, and runs through to the back of the oven. The elevation in figure 36 shows how it is suggested the arch finish at the inner row of bricks in the double brick back wall. To determine its form, it is possible to construct a timber former as was done for the doorway. This would be left in place until the end of construction, when it would be burned out. An easier method is to form the shape with sand. Fill the oven chamber with a pile of damp sand, well tamped, and shape a curve from side to side. The crown of the vault will rest on the topside of the doorway arch. The elevation in figure 33 shows the form it will take.

To be certain of the shape of the arch, figure 34 shows a way of establishing the curve. On a vertical wall or board insert drawing pins at aa. Their distance is the span of the arch. Ensure they are level. Mark a point b below them, the distance shown (230mm). That is the height of the arch. Suspend a string from the two drawing pins with its lowest point at the mark b. It will follow the curve indicated. Transfer this curve onto pieces of stiff cardboard, or thin ply or hardboard. Cut them to shape. These may be inserted vertically into the pile of sand, resting their ends on the third course of bricks, and will give an exact guide to the shape the sand should take. They may be left in the sand while building is underway.

Figure 33: section through the oven (A—A in figure 31), showing the shape of the main vault and its relationship to the oven doorway arch (scale 1:20).

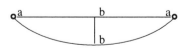

Figure 34: drawing the curve of the oven vault, using a string and two drawing pins. aa measures 990mm; bb measures 230mm.

The bricks for the vault are laid lengthwise on edge, as they were for the doorway arch. When installing them, stagger the joints between courses, as if it were a brick wall.

Once all the bricks are in place, with sufficient mortar between them to maintain their respective angles – remember too that the bricks should not actually touch each other, there should be mortar between each one – an external coating of mortar can be applied to the arch as a whole. Let the initial installation go off over half a day or a night, then pack the joints well with fresh mortar and skim a thin layer of mortar over the entire outside. Add a further layer of mortar of approximately 10mm and leave to dry and set.

There will be a gaping hole at the far end between the top of the third course of bricks and the curve of the arch. However, as the arch finishes with the first brick of the double brick wall at the end, there is every chance to tidy up the outward appearance and secure the join. Fill the aperture as tidily as possible with bricks laid at right angles to the wall, trying not to let too much mortar spill on to the inside. It is easiest if this end is constructed in tandem with the making of the arch. Once the arch is completed, the outer skin of bricks can be finished off plumb and true. This is shown in figure 36.

Similarly, the interstice at the front of the oven, between the door arch and the main vault of the oven should be filled with cut bricks and mortar.

When the arch has been finally plastered, the oven chamber itself is complete. It is also filled with sand. Leave it several days before emptying the sand with a small shovel.

Figure 35 is a side elevation of the oven chamber before the superstructure is begun.

The Scottish baker, John White of Dunbar, wrote in 1828 of the cement required for turning the arch over the oven, commenting that often too limey a mortar caused lime to fall upon the bread in the baking. His specific was a mortar of blood and lime: 'procure as much well burnt lime-shell (the whiter the better) as will be sufficient for the purpose; reduce that shell into a powder, and put it through a fine sieve. In the next place, procure some bullocks blood, newly drawn, mix as much of the lime powder in the blood as will bring it to the consistence of a thin paste, then dip the dressed stones or bricks, one by one, in this paste and lay them in their regular course, till the whole is finished. A very little of this cement must be made at a time, as it soon gets too stiff for working.'

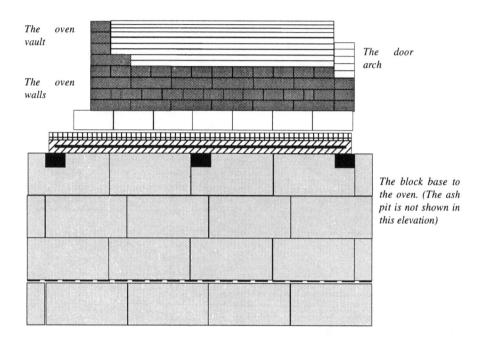

The oven vault

The door arch

The oven walls

The block base to the oven. (The ash pit is not shown in this elevation)

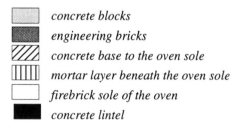 concrete blocks

engineering bricks

concrete base to the oven sole

mortar layer beneath the oven sole

firebrick sole of the oven

concrete lintel

Figure 35: a side view of the oven, including the base, the concrete, mortar and firebrick sole, the oven itself and its vaulted roof (scale 1:20).

0 10 20 30 40 50 60 70 80 90 100 110 120 130cm

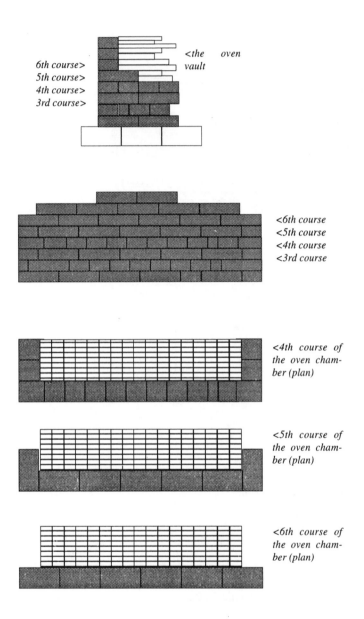

6th course>
5th course>
4th course>
3rd course>

<the   oven
vault

<6th course
<5th course
<4th course
<3rd course

<4th course of
the oven cham-
ber (plan)

<5th course of
the oven cham-
ber (plan)

<6th course of
the oven cham-
ber (plan)

*Figure 36: side elevation, end elevation and plans of the later courses in engineering
bricks to be built at the end of the oven vault (scale 1:20).*

0   10   20   30   40   50   60   70   80   90   100   110   120   130cm

Building the upper outer walls and the chimney

This is the last phase of the main structure, it includes both brick and block work. The outer walls (which are in block work) are put up at the same time as the chimney, which they are tied into.

The sixth course of blocks (counting up from the foundation) is shown in figure 37. The bricks marked (a) in the plan are engineering bricks that act as the connecting pad between the chimney stack and the oven chamber itself.

Succeeding illustrations (figures 38 to 41) show the progress of the work, with each brick and block detailed in its correct position. The front of the chimney stack is supported on a concrete lintel that is easily installed spanning the side walls that stretch up from the sides of the ash pit.

A second lintel is inserted at the back of the chimney stack to take the weight of the superstructure off the doorway arch (better safe than sorry).

Once that has been installed, it should be plain sailing, provided bricks are level and everything is plumb. Common bricks have been specified for the chimney stack, but facing bricks would be more handsome, or good secondhand treasures even better.

The chimney pot is an item that can add much to the appearance. Antiques are worth searching out. It will be more secure if it has a square base than can slot into the brick flue before the cement flaunching is plastered round the base.

Insulation

The oven chamber occupies but a portion of the square box that has been raised around it. The rest of the volume is filled with insulation. As the principle of operation is heat retention, it is evidently self-defeating if the heat so ardently created evaporates into thin air before you have time to profit from it. The more insulation, therefore, the better.

Modern materials such as glass-fibre and vermiculite are very effective, but more costly than plain builders' sand. Efficiency may be enhanced, but cost controlled, by mixing sand and vermiculite.

Whichever material you elect, it is heaped over the crest of the oven vault to a depth of at least 500mm at its highest point.

There were earlier recipes for efficient insulation. Richard Bacon, who has written of restoring brick ovens in the USA, quotes Catherine Beecher's

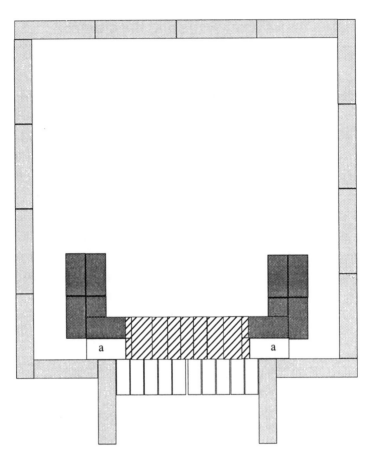

concrete blocks (100mm)

engineering bricks

the door arch (plan)

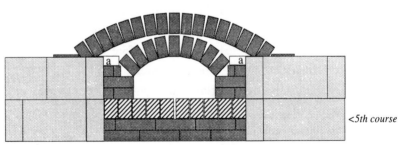

<5th course

Figure 37: plan and front elevation of the sixth course of blocks showing the first brick of the chimney stack, marked a *(scale 1:20). Only the front of the oven is detailed.*

0   10   20   30   40   50   60   70   80   90   100 110 120 130cm

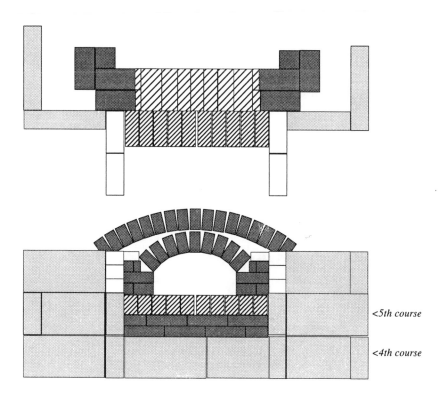

<5th course

<4th course

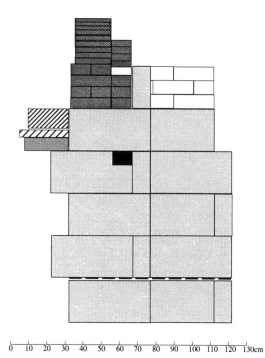

Figure 38: plan, front and side elevations showing the brick and block work needed for the sixth course of blocks, counting up from the foundation (scale 1:20).

concrete blocks

engineering bricks

common bricks

concrete lintel

firebricks

mortar base

concrete base

0 10 20 30 40 50 60 70 80 90 100 110 120 130cm

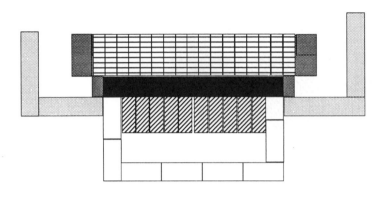

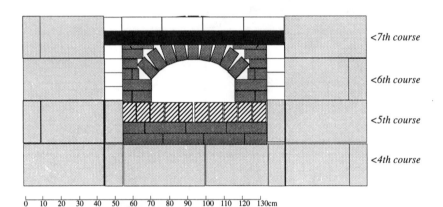

<7th course

<6th course

<5th course

<4th course

0 10 20 30 40 50 60 70 80 90 100 110 120 130cm

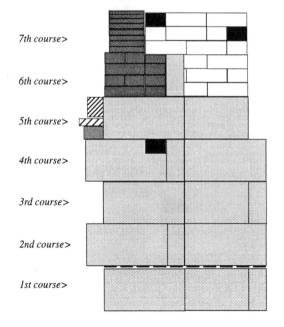

7th course>

6th course>

5th course>

4th course>

3rd course>

2nd course>

1st course>

Figure 39: plan, front and side elevations showing the brick and blockwork needed for the seventh course of blocks, counting up from the foundation (scale 1:20).

	concrete blocks
	engineering bricks
	common bricks
	concrete lintel
	firebricks
	mortar base
	concrete base

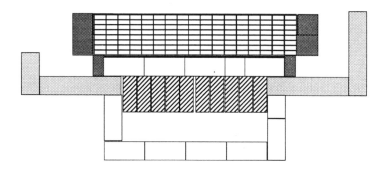

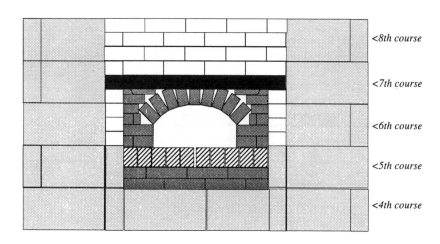

<8th course

<7th course

<6th course

<5th course

<4th course

0 10 20 30 40 50 60 70 80 90 100 110 120 130cm

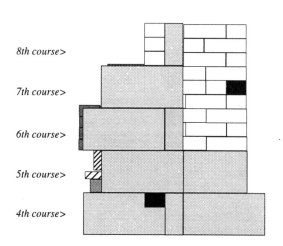

8th course>

7th course>

6th course>

5th course>

4th course>

Figure 40: plan, front and side elevations showing the brick and blockwork needed for the eighth course of blocks, counting up from the foundation (scale 1:20).

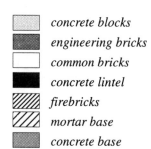

concrete blocks

engineering bricks

common bricks

concrete lintel

firebricks

mortar base

concrete base

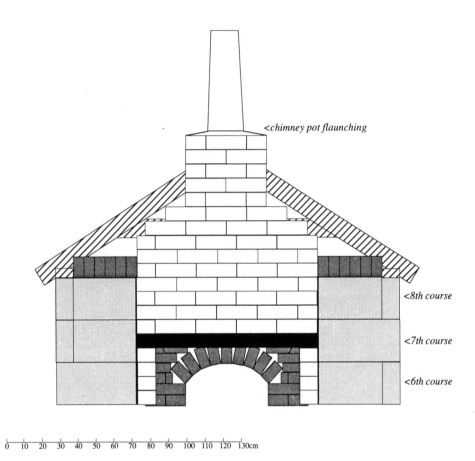

<chimney pot flaunching

<8th course

<7th course

<6th course

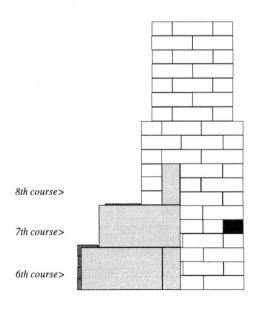

8th course>

7th course>

6th course>

*Figure 41: front and side eleva-
tions showing the brickwork for
the upper part of the chimney
stack (scale 1:20).*

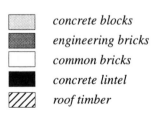

concrete blocks

engineering bricks

common bricks

concrete lintel

roof timber

Domestic Receipt-Book which recommends that 'after the arch is formed [over the oven], four or five bushels of ashes are spread over it, and then a covering of charcoal over that, then another layer of bricks over-all. The use of this is, that the ashes become heated, and the charcoal being a non-conductor, the heat is retained for much longer.'

The roof

A later section discusses variations to finish and surface treatment, but some form of roof or waterproofing is essential. The sand that now envelops the oven is absorbent stuff, and long hours of burning will be wasted if the structure gets too damp.

The elevation in figure 41 shows a timber frame for a roof made out of 100 x 50mm softwood. Depending on the roofing material chosen, there should be two or three of these frames. They rest on small timber wall plates of the same section, screwed into the tops of the blocks, or attached with metal ties sold at the builders' merchants for that purpose (in which case the wall plates would have to be fixed before you fill the void with sand).

The rafters are each set at an angle of 32° from the horizontal, giving an angle of 116° at the apex. The length of each main rafter is approximately 1200mm. Consult a building trades manual if you wish to construct anything more complicated than a boarded and felted, or tin roof.

Simplicity of construction has determined that the roof should not wrap around the chimney stack. Although some weatherproofing is necessary, it need not be major league. However, this leaves the front wall of the oven uncrested, and I suggest you finish it with some halved engineering bricks laid on edge, bedded in mortar. These are shown in figure 41. The gable at the other end of the roof may be made fast with weather boarding or planking backed with felt. An open gable at the chimney end does mean that cats can doze the day away in the warmth of yesterday's firing, and that there is a useful space for putting rakes and peels.

How the roof is finished may depend on location, finance, aesthetics and enthusiasm. Slates or tiles are the obvious, and laborious, answer, but roofing-felt on plywood would serve the purpose, as would corrugated iron or some form of metal sheeting. Gutters might be thought gilding the lily.

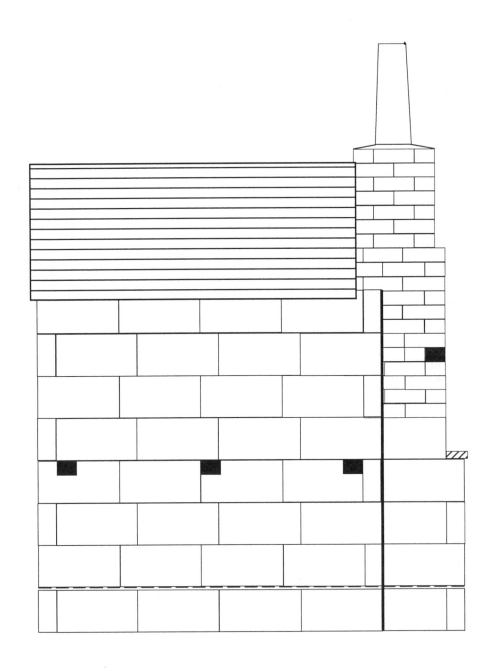

Figure 42: a side elevation of the completed oven (scale 1:20)

The work top

As it is, the ash pit is open at the top, but although an ample slot is required so that the embers and ashes can be raked out of the oven directly into the pit below the threshold, there is also room for a useful counter. The most elegant object might be a piece of marble or slate rescued from a rubbish tip or flea market that can be rested on the block at the top of the ash pit, and on a strip of iron that can be bedded into the mortar before you place the cheek blocks that make up the fifth course (see above). Alternatively, you can use a couple of concrete slabs. It should be noted that it is frequently the case that a fire is raked out when still burning quite merrily. This may occur because the firing of the oven has lagged behing the development of the dough, and you are in desperate need of oven space if the loaves are not to over-prove. The blaze in the ash pit, therefore, can be fierce, and the work surface, be it marble, slate or concret, may get well heated. Experience has shown that marble and slate will often crack in these temperatures. Concrete slabs are more stable. Enthusiastic gardeners once took to sterilising their soil in microwave ovens. However, the stones that were often in the humus would crack and splinter as the microwaves heated the air trapped in pockets inside. The process became somewhat explosive, even dangerous. Perhaps there is a moral here.

Outside finishes

The building erected is of concrete blocks: none the most attractive of finishes. It is likely, therefore, that some improvement will be wanted. Paint is easy, but perhaps rejected in favour of something more considered. Cement render may be the next candidate, though requiring some practice before perfect smoothness and adhesion is achieved. This render may be textured if the Tyrolean effect, or the pebble-dashed, is something which pleases. Alternatively, a further layer or weatherproof material may be applied: ceramic tiles, or slates or tiles hung on battens. The possibilities are infinite. Read the next chapter for more radical actions.

Incidentals

There are two items without which the oven will function poorly. First, a door. Early accounts of using brick ovens often refer to stopping the door with a flour paste, or mud, underlining the necessity of a tight seal to the orifice. This probably reflects that the oven in question was small, therefore heat loss could be rapid, and that baking times were long (see below) and the initial temperature none too high. These would demand a close-fitting stopper to minimise any loss of heat.

It is not so absolutely necessary with the oven described here. For one, it is comparatively large for the load that will be put on it and the doorway opening is relatively small for the volume of the interior. For another, our baking times are generally shorter. For a third, most of the heat is radiant, i.e. is stored in and given off by the brick walls and roof. Although rapid exhalation of the heat is not to be encouraged, more can be squandered than in a cooler oven. However, some means of closure is required. Some variations in design are shown in figure 43, which is taken from American examples of old farmstead ovens. The neatest may be a well-hung cast iron door with hinges set in the masonry. This is not beyond a competent metal worker, it just needs forward planning. Commercial ovens often had and have doors that slid vertically open and shut in the manner of the guillotine, or roller shutters that work like a Victorian secretaire or roller-top desk. While those are more difficult, a guillotine-like rise and fall is possible to engineer, as there is space in the flue above for the door when open, and there is space on the sides of the doorway for the metal guides.

A more direct solution is an iron plate that is lifted into place, and this is certainly cheap to manufacture, and effective. It merely needs a stay or legs to keep it vertically against the door surround.

A large baulk of timber is also a possibility. However, it does start to char in the heat of a just-raked oven, and it will need regular replacement.

If the oven is only used for pizzas, then a door is not needed at all.

The second item that will soon become essential is some reliable method of determining temperature. The question of when the oven has been sufficiently fired, and other vexed matters of running the whole process of heating and baking will be be dealt with later, but a thermometer is a good place to start.

It is possible to build in access for a temperature probe by inserting a small conduit from the outside of the oven wall to the oven chamber itself. The thermometer can be inserted through this conduit during the baking period and a digital read-out can display the temperature. This will depend on preplanning during construction.

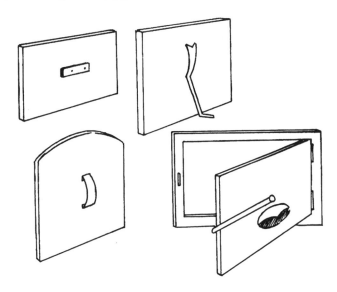

Figure 43: studies of different door designs, based on Richard Bacon's findings from old ovens in New England (see bibliography). An iron plate with stay or stays, as depicted at top right, is the simplest and sturdiest pattern.

It is also possible to buy an oven thermometer – reading up to 600°F – that can be placed in the oven once the fire has been raked out. This is quite enough for most people's needs.

While the fire is actually burning, no instrument will tell you whether you have burned long enough – that's for experience and observation.

Architectural vapours

The preceding account of the oven's construction makes plain the essence of the instrument is reducible to an hermetically sealed box that can be vented during firing. Foundations, chimneys, roofs and external finishes are optional trappings. Hence the design I have described is but one, not necessarily elegant, answer to the question: how do I make this box serviceable and long-lasting?

Visitors to the River Café in west London – a fine restaurant serving Italian food where a partner is wife of the architect Sir Richard Rogers – can gaze with awe at the dull gleam of the severe stainless-steel floor-to-ceiling facade of an oven that is vented invisibly and whose only apparent working part is a square black hole cut in the middle of a pristine sheet. Contrast this with the American poet, W.S. Merwin's account of an oven in his garden in rural France: 'a small Romanesque apse, a formal cave in the open, floating through the centuries like an ark on a river, ... stone slabs of limestone broad as table tops, pile up in the shape of a straw beehive.' Same oven, different clothes.

Or in the Western Desert in the Second World War, where men still needed bread to fight, there were no architectural beauties, nor historical gems, but empty oil drums, buried in sand and given a chimney pipe. These camp ovens performed miracles. As they do today if you go to a hippy festival in the open air in England over the summer months.

Even if identical principles of design are followed as in what might be termed the Prospect oven, there is still an infinity of routes to arrive at the desired end. We specified concrete blocks, but they could as easily (though more slowly and expensively) have been bricks. Sir Winston Churchill was famously addicted to bricklaying, so might be the reader.

Equally feasible is to construct the oven's envelope from stone, thus creating a nearer facsimile of those ovens of the Dordogne that catch the holiday maker's imagination. Again, the task will be longer, and perhaps more expensive, but all problems of external beauty will be solved. A stone finish can be applied to the blocks, as a thin (150mm or 300mm) facing, just as you might add a brick skin. This would increase the insulating envelope as well as making a handsome object, but the labour involved might cause you to question using the concrete blocks in the first place.

Another aesthetic may approve of a brutalist conclusion of poured concrete with the shuttering marks proudly revealed, or the surface polished to adamantine marble. These are suggestions of an amateur architect, not baker.

Once accepting the oven's underlying principle, it may also be possible that readers have some existing building or structure that can be adapted with little effort, and no danger. I think particularly of old privies or masonry garden sheds, or perhaps an outbuilding such as used to house the copper boiler. I once heard of, though never visited, a brick oven that was built inside the outside lavatory of a terraced house in Newcastle.

These buildings would be admirable for conversion: they may even be large enough to give the baker shelter as well as the oven. Were they to be adapted, the points to watch would be that the foundations and under-floor slab are sufficient, and that there is no risk of fire to the roof or neighbouring buildings. Ventilation may need more thought than before. There would be little charm in stoking an oven in a room filled with dense smoke.

Figure 45 is a schematic presentation of the Prospect oven with the roof extended over the chimney breast and supported on two pillars to give weather-protected working space. To achieve this, one would need do no more than extend the wall plates from the oven to the pillars, perhaps thickening them up a little (depending on the roof covering), and manufacture more of the trusses that are shown in figure 41.

Another scheme might be as shown in figure 18 where the oven is overarched by a canopy. This oven, part of a Mediterranean 'summer kitchen', has been contained within a complete box, giving a useful flat surface for storage on its top. The chimney and flue are contained within the structure, with ventilation being closed off by a damper above the oven door. This arrangement has much to recommend it. The oven door can be very small, thus reducing heat loss, as its only function, other than admitting the food, is to provide draught for the fire. The doorway of the oven under discussion in this book, however, has to make room for exhaust as well as inhalation.

A roof is not the only form of weatherproofing. A Mohammedan look to the oven might be given by finishing the top with a dome of cement. Once the oven is built, and the sand has been poured round to give insulation, it can be moulded into the form of a dome. Take a sheet of plywood approximately 1200mm square. Using one corner as the centre, draw a quarter-circle with a radius equivalent to half the distance from side wall to side wall of the oven. Cut along this line. Ensure the sand around the oven has been generously heaped, moistened and well tamped down. Find the centre point of this heap by stretching two lines across the diagonals. Insert a long pivot at this point. Holding the board in both hands, rotate it round the pivot, sweeping away the surplus sand as you go.

The dome shape once created, keep it damp and plaster it with a 25mm coat of lime mortar such as was used for the rest of the construction. When this has begun to go off, stick chicken wire or plastic-coated garden wire-netting to follow the shape. Plaster with a further 25mm coat. Finish with a thin third coat of very strong cement to make it waterproof. The illustrations in figure 44 may help.

Embellishment may know no bounds – Swiss chalet, Gothic hermitage, Classical shrine: all grist to the mill of those who want.

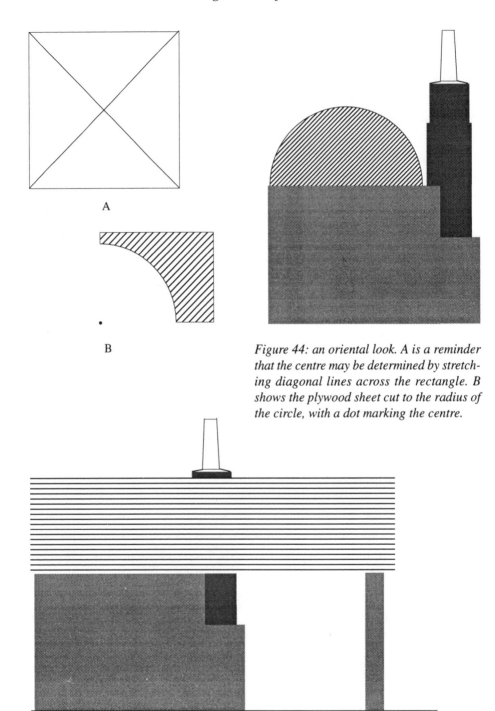

A

B

Figure 44: an oriental look. A is a reminder that the centre may be determined by stretching diagonal lines across the rectangle. B shows the plywood sheet cut to the radius of the circle, with a dot marking the centre.

Figure 45: side elevation of an oven with roof extended over the working area, supported by pillars (scale 1:40).

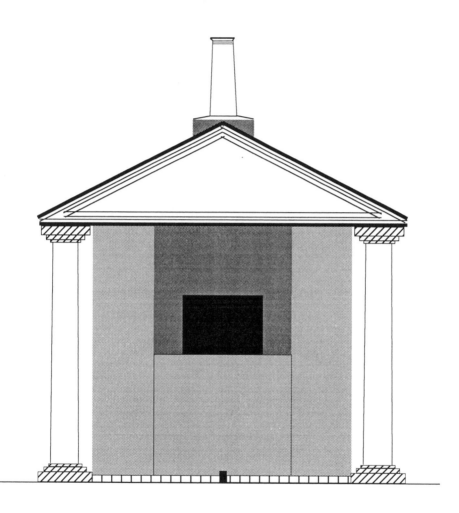

Figure 46: a classical treatment for the formal garden.

Prefabricated ovens

The history of the manufactured oven is long. A domed shape could be made in pottery, installed in a suitable hole in the masonry fireplace, then plastered into permanent position. The high-fired pottery withstood any temperature a domestic blaze could produce and until some major breakage occurred, it was cleaner to operate. In Britain, the most important places of manufacture were the north Devon towns of Bideford, Fremington and Barnstaple, where cloam ovens were made from gravel-tempered clay – which 'opened up the fine-textured Fremington clay to enable it to dry right through and reduce the time and temperature needed for firing, … and were reckoned stronger and more heat-resistant in use', says Alison Grant, the historian of the north Devon pottery industry. A report of their existence in 1716 noted that they were more fuel efficient than brick ovens. They were manufactured by the firm of Brannam, which survives today, who also produced cloam scalding pans for the manufacture of clotted cream.

They were made in several sizes: from 2 pecks to 12 pecks (which is large) from the early modern period right through to this century. Barnstaple had strong links with the Americas and the tobacco trade (it also manufactured pipes). Devon ovens, therefore, are found in equal number on the other side of the Atlantic, just as they can be found here in the south west, and, for example, in south Wales. (Alison Grant cites a study of the Welsh examples by Eurwyn William in *Medieval and Later Pottery in Wales*, 1979.) Enthusiasts have been able to find them in antique shops, even in recent years. The cloam ovens were usually built into the fabric of the house, but the eighteenth-century traveller Dr. Richard Pococke recorded their use as hearth-set ovens, as if a pot oven: 'being heated they stop 'em over with embers to keep in the heat.'

The potters would cut the door out of the formed oven before it was fired, so the purchaser would have the complete kit when he bought it at the hardware store (Figures 47 and 48). When they were set into masonry, one of the Brannams is quoted as saying in 1921, the preference was bed the oven in 'a mixture prepared from road scrapings, if of a clayey nature, with plenty of horse droppings well mixed and worked up, for there was no fear in those days of the deteriorating effect of tar and oil. A layer of this mixture 1 1/2 inches thick was first put down and the oven floated on level: the whole was then covered with about one inch layer of the mixture, which in practice

Figure 47: a drawing of a cloam oven, taken in 1922, with its door in place.

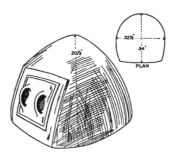

Figure 48: studies of a terracotta oven, from drawings of a Devon cloam oven by Alan Scott.

Figure 49: ovens do not have to be set in one place. This late medieval picture of a portable oven shows it at rest outside a baker's stall, the telltale twisted bretzels hanging on the pole above the door.

would all bake up and so form a second oven or casing which retained the heat. Brick or stone masonry built over and around, at least twelve inches thick, completed the operations.'

Such ovens are still available in north Africa and Portugal today. The German miller and baker Rolf Peter Weichold brought one to my home in Devon one summer and we encased it in mud on a section of hard-standing and baked a passable, though haphazard, loaf therein.

More professional, certainly on a grander scale, are the sectional terracotta ovens that are supplied by several manufacturers in Europe, particularly with an eye to the country farm restorer, or the seeker after the good life, and the pizza trade – especially those restaurants where the appeal of an open oven is central to their operation. Firms in France such as Fours Grand-Mère – Tisserant & Georges, 2 rue de la Gare, 88700 Jeanménil, or Saint-Jacques Industries, ZI de la Grave, 06510 Carros provide these, as do the Italian firm of Foco of Genoa. Their sizes vary, from as little as one metre square, to twice that.

Were one to install such a prefabricated oven, the procedure would be little different from that already described, except the bother of building the oven chamber itself would be saved. It would still require insulation and protection from the weather.

Figure 50: a detail from an engraving in the manual of bakery by Malouin, Description et détails des arts du meunier, du vermicelier et du boulanger… *(1761–7). This is a large round oven, for commercial use, with emplacement for a water boiler on the left. Hot water was essential for the controlled production of bread.*

RUNNING THE OVEN

Construction is but half the battle. Once over, an essential preliminary is to season the building by letting it dry slowly, then heating it a little and often until residual moisture is driven from the materials – mortar and fresh buildings, like cucumbers, are largely water. Leave it for a while, then burn small fires for a week or ten days, at any convenient time. After that, a few practice firings may be undertaken when loaves can be baked, but without illusions: they will be burned, undercooked or otherwise spoiled. During these practices, watch for indicators of temperature during firing, then monitor the heat of all parts of the oven once the fire is raked out and during all subsequent procedures. Experience is the main factor in successful baking.

It will not be possible to run a brick oven without wood. Coal is probably not a real option nowadays. Northern and western districts may supply peat, but I have no experience of it myself, save noticing that many Scottish bakers once burned it in their ovens.

When we were still an agricultural nation, with vast reservoirs of manpower in the fields, wood took many forms. Medieval commoners in the dales of Yorkshire had rights to gather brushwood or ling for their ovens. The writer W.S. Merwin, mentioned above, records that his French oven was fuelled with cut brambles. Others have relied on furze, ferns and gorse. However, the medieval bakers of London were forbidden by their Guild to use stubble, straw, fern or reeds (and London provides an early evidence of the use of coal as fuel). When coppicing was a way of life for whole families, and hedging was done with a bill-hook not a mechanical flail, then bundles of trimmings were done up in faggots and sold for burning. Cook, if she had an open hearth, would throw a faggot on the flames, and the baker would fire his oven with one. If bought betimes and stored until dry, they burned fiercely and fast. It is clear that bakers used often to use two sorts of wood fuel: faggots and 'spokes'. At the end of the eighteenth century, faggots were supplied into London at 26 shillings per 100, while spokes were sold at 20 shillings per 100, and were logs large enough to be split in two before burning.

An inventory dated 1587, taken at the death of one Robert Symons, a baker of Banbury, underlines the importance of wood to the pursuance of the craft. He had two hovels filled with faggots in his yard, plus other timber and firewood worth £7, while in the barn was stacked a rick of furze on top of great timber baulks – the whole worth £10. As his day's stock in the shop, 27 dozen loaves 'of all sortes', was counted as worth but £1 7s. 0d., his capital tied up in fuel was not inconsiderable. The parsonical diarist from Essex, Ralph Josselin wrote in 1678 of his pleasure in clearing 'Chalkeney wood of my share. poles. tits. longwood, without any considerable hurt to beast, waggon, and none to man.' 'Tits' was an Essex dialect word meaning faggots for the oven. Such categories of wood were recognised in other countries, at other times. The anonymous *Journal d'un Bourgeois de Paris* notes, in a catalogue of horrors suffered by that city, that in 1418 wood was bitterly expensive: 'small firewood such as that from Marne, still green, was 40 s. *parisis* or three francs the hundred; measured logs, 12 s. the measure; wretched faggots, nothing but leaves, 36 s. *parisis* a hundred.'

With no cheap workforce available in the woods today, we have either to cut our own timber, laboriously; to buy it, expensively; or scrounge around for industrial or commercial waste (the modern version of coppicing). Buying timber, unless in large quantities, makes the oven dear to run, but there are some industries that use the heart, but discard the half-round off-cuts when they plank whole tree-trunks. For instance, factories manufacturing pallets often sell bundles of these offcuts for very competitive prices. Over the course of a few years, I have depended on pallet-makers, fencing contractors, blackboard manufacturers, and builders' skip operators for regular and cheap supplies of offcuts or rejected materials. The woods have either been fast-grown softwoods, medium density fibreboard – quick and easy burning, but pernicious dust – or general builders' discards, including painted and treated boards and generous quantities of nails, screws and bolts.

The combustion temperature is high enough to negate harmful residues in timber you obtain by whatever means. It also burns off any resins or flavour enhancers that might otherwise linger on the bricks themselves. Therefore the taste of the bread does not alter according to the fuel burned. However, if pizzas are being cooked in an oven where the fire is left smouldering at the back or sides during the actual cooking, it might be wise to be sure of the chemical cleanliness of the wood used: no paints, varnish, timber treatments, etc. I treasure accounts of the celebrated Parisian baker Lionel Poilâne whose ovens are fuelled by boxes and scavengings from the markets and factories of industrial Paris. One advantage of using secondhand timber is that it is dry and will therefore burn faster.

Figure 51: a drawing based on a French woodcut from the seventeenth century which shows the wood stored beneath the oven, the peel standing to one side, and the loaves proving on a bench. A bed in the bakery might be warm, but would be fume-filled. One presumes this was artist's licence.

Although logs supplied by the log man for winter fires are a distinct, if ruinous, possibility, they display many drawbacks. They will invariably need long storage to be properly dry; they will often be hardwood, thus take longer to get going, even if calorifically more efficient. Long timbers, yet thin, are the best.

Bakers used to store wood under the oven itself, and would often load the oven with tomorrow's fuel at the end of a day's baking. This practice was usually condemned, as the roughly handled logs would damage the sole and the brickwork. It is a method that may be tried, but there is no substitute for obtaining adequate supplies of fuel and holding them out of the weather for a decent period of time.

Many descriptions of firing ovens survive – some are quoted to great effect by Elizabeth David. As preliminary to our own account of acceptable current practice, here are some counsels from the French eighteenth-century author, Antoine Parmentier, writing in 1778.

He observes that any fuel may be used, including dead leaves and plant stalks, but that a clear, bright flame is necessary to heat the vault of the oven, with ample cinders and embers to heat the sole – hence wood is best. He distinguishes between the various parts of the oven, each being heated by different stages of the firing – he is talking of a larger oven than we treat of here, something in the region of four metres long, and oval in shape. To begin, place a large faggot across the back of the oven, held off the floor either by virtue of its twisted shape, or supported on small chocks, so the flames can circulate above and below. Using this as a base, two more faggots are leant against it, running lengthwise. A second pair are piled on top, their ends reaching to the edges of the sides. This arrangement, called the *charge*, is ignited at the far end of the oven, by means of a burning ember or firebrand (see figure 52). Once the fire is merrily burning, the baker should adjust the faggots and spread the embers so that one part of the sole is not heated at the expense of others. This major blaze, however, will not be sufficient to complete the entire job. When it has reduced the faggots to ash and cinder, these are removed to the ash pit and a second fire built nearer the oven door. This consists of faggots cut in half, piled criss-cross as was the first. Beware, he advises, of building it too close to the door, otherwise the spritely flames will shoot straight up the chimney, wasting their heat, and setting light to the soot. Build it about one third way into the oven. As it burns down, so the baker moves it towards the front, to heat the doorway itself. The procedure described relates to the first heating, but in the course of the working day,

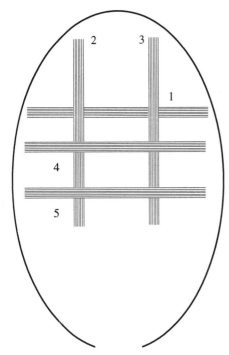

Figure 52: the order of placing faggots for the first, main, firing, according to Parmentier.

successive fires will have to be constructed in order to keep the oven up to scratch. In these, the baker subdivides his faggots, makes sure the wood is all small-sectioned, and lights the fire at the sides of the oven rather than at the back. As firing follows firing, so the amount of wood reduces. If there is a dead time, when the oven is not needed nor a fire required, he counsels that wood for the next blaze be put in place. Subjected to all that residual heat, it soon gets to the point where ignition will be immediate and fierce, thus shortening the time needed for one of these supplementary firings.

Our own routine is less elaborate; the oven is but a fraction the size, and we do not have to cope with the press of successive bakings, nor irate customers waiting for their breakfast loaf.

A typical day's baking, fine and dry in the summer when the oven has been used regularly two days a week, starts after lunch at two in the afternoon when the first flames are kindled. The fuel is builders' discards: mostly soft wood, well seasoned. A vigorous fire is started, using small-sectioned choppings, at the front of the oven. It is fed after 30 or 40 minutes with 8 or 10 more substantial pieces. When these have burned, they will leave a bed of embers that act as motor to the ensuing refuellings. The fire is left to its own devices for two hours, until 5 pm, when it is fed again with a substantial armful of baulks up to 150 x 75 mm in section, and perhaps 1 metre in length. At this juncture, the dough is made – a simple yeasted dough, enough to make 8 loaves each weighing 600g.

The fire burns unattended for the next 3 hours, when it is given a final present of four or five slight timbers at 8 o'clock in the evening. The main period of burning has seen the flames pass from the front to the back of the oven. The last refuelling bolsters the embers that are heating the furthest corners. At this stage, it is possible that the front of the sole has been devoid of hot ash and ember for several hours, so the burning coals may be spread evenly over the whole floor to ensure that everything has had equal attention.

The dough is knocked back at 9 o'clock and an hour later, at 10, the oven is raked out and the door closed to give a chance for the heat to soak into the structure: rather as you leave a piece of meat to rest after roasting so that it becomes suffused with pink rather than dark red in parts and brown in others. A temperature gauge is left inside to check on progress. The oven heat is just below 600°F.

At 10.30 pm the loaves are moulded and put in tins or baskets for their final proof. The oven heat is 550°F. An hour later it is 500°F, and at midnight it is

450°F. The loaves are ready for the oven. This is swept out, but not scuffled (see below), and the bread inserted.

The heat drops immediately, to about 350°F, but recovers by the end of baking (20 minutes), to 425°F. At 10 o'clock the next morning, 12 hours after the fire was raked out, the internal temperature is still 225°F.

This is a relaxed way of doing it. It is always wisest to have the oven wait for the bread, not the reverse. The times I give here are those of a particular day and night of working. The oven was heated for a sufficient time to get the whole fabric warmed, the heat was therefore gradually released. Had the burning time been shorter, a fair temperature might have been obtained, but for less time. The slow fall of heat may be accelerated by repeated opening of the oven door and loading further items to be cooked. Nothing absorbs heat like cold food. This makes planning for two or more batches of bread or other items more complicated than the straight-line temperature graph leads us to suppose. If serial cooking is required from a single heating, choose things that track the oven's cooling. Start with breads, follow with cakes, finish with stews. Although the oven will pass comparatively rapidly through the upper temperature registers – the sort of heat needed to give a fine crackle to the crust – it will sit on the middle band for several hours.

Given the flames pass from back to front (seeking the fresh air), it would make sense to follow Parmentier's advice on building the fire as in the illustration. However, this is more complicated when dealing with scrappy wood than it is with faggots. What may be more important is that the fire is allowed to burn most of the time, rather than smokily smoulder. This means building it with small stuff until it has a real heat at its heart. Once various critical points are reached, combustion becomes quicker and quicker. Potters who have wood-fired kilns, working to far greater temperatures than bakers, tell of nights spent thrusting great logs into the flames, only to see them spontaneously dissolve in a puff of smoke and flame, so fierce is the heat.

The invariable desire of flames for the open air and oxygen imposes certain limitations on how a front-vented oven is stoked. Imagine that the first half of the firing is over, that there is a fair bed of embers at the front of the oven, but several logs towards the rear that have not yet burned. If fresh fuel is inserted, it will inevitably burn first nearest the door, leaving the nethermost parts still barely warmed. It is more effective therefore, if each substantial refuelling is allowed to burn itself to charcoal, contributing towards the stock of hot coals that will eventually cover the floor in its entirety.

If the firing is long, and use of fuel profligate, there will certainly be time enough to move the glowing coals from one part of the oven to the next in order to ensure even heating. If insufficient attention is paid to the minutiae of firing, it is almost certain that a simple and small batch of loaves will cook satisfactorily, but less sure that ambitious procedures will be successful. Perhaps a full load is wanted: the front of the oven will often be less hot than the back. Perhaps two batches are needed, in quick succession. This is possible on the heat curve that I have described above, but timing is critical. The doughs have to come together at exactly the right time, especially the second batch. The oven will probably not be hot enough to 'rescue' an overproved loaf. This works better with practice.

The operation of the original wood-fired oven built and used by Andrew Whitley at the Village Bakery at Melmerby in Cumbria shows how relatively trouble-free such an instrument can be. The fire is on the side, as in figure 15, and is stoked at the end of the working day. Refreshed halfway through the evening, it burns for the rest of the night until baking commences early the next morning. By way of contrast, Andrew Whitley has also installed a *gueulard* oven, of French design (see figure 17). This has a separate fire that can be kept alive through baking and kindled at a moment's notice to reheat the oven between loads.

An oven such as the one under discussion here is less easily refreshed than a gueulard. Once a bake is finished, then a fire can be rekindled, but without forced draught, the process is never short. This will generally mean that it needs reloading with bread too soon, when the heat is called 'flash', and has not really soaked into the structure, but merely caressed the reflective surfaces.

These strictures serve to underline that wood-fired ovens perform differently from a modern electric or oil-fired machine. Each baker knew the hot and cool spots, but many were the miscalculations. Perhaps the dough was ready too soon, thus charged when the oven was too hot: all burned today. Or the fire was not spread properly over the sole: all doughy. Or the apprentice put the loaves too near the side walls: burned again. (They used to put spacers down the sides of large ovens so that tins were not pressed tight against the walls.) Finally, as heat was ineluctably falling all the day through, early bakes might be crusty, and later ones light. Those were the days when your father would send you to the baker with a very specific set of demands as to hardness and appearance: no longer.

Figure 53: an oven in an eighteenth-century French bakery, from the Encyclopédie. *The baker is using a rooker to adjust the fire. A peel is stored above his head. The oven door is on the floor at the left. The flue is outside the oven mouth which vents into the cowl.*

Figure 54: bread preparation in the same bakery. Next to the mountain of dough on the table is a scraper for cleaning work surfaces, and a flat scraper for the dough. The trough lid can be seen pinned back to the wall by the clip labelled C. Long cloths for keeping the loaves apart during final proof are hanging from the hook by the window on the right.

Stoking the fire, and cleaning the oven afterwards, needs equipment. A bow saw and an axe for the timber, an ash box for the embers, a poker, bellows, a rake, perhaps a shovel, and a scuffle or mop. The ash box is already built into our design, but if a variation is constructed, its necessity should be borne in mind. The French called it an *étouffoir*, smotherer or extinguisher, and it was a copper box with tight fitting lid which took all the ash and embers as they were removed from the oven. By virtue of its lid, the flames would be soon damped and the baker could extract the charcoal for the fire next day. An open ash pit has no such advantages, for the fire continues until all is burned – and should it be necessary to rake out the oven before everything has been consumed by flames, then the fire in the ash pit is merry indeed. However, the ash which is left is excellent feed for the garden. On some farms in Devon, there are free-standing ash houses: ashes from the winter fires were stored to be spread on the fields come spring, or used as lye, for soap-making.

A poker may be necessary to rearrange the burning logs. It sometimes happens that too large a baulk finds its way to the bottom and side of the fire. Combustion will be very slow unless it is lifted off the sole to allow the heat to play on every side. In Yorkshire, this tool was called a 'fruggin', being 'a pole to stir in the oven when it is heated to stir the ashes up'.

Bellows may be useful to provoke a bit of action in the fire department, however, most have short reach and will be no help at the back of the oven. I hold in reserve a length of copper pipe and can sometimes be seen puffing vainly into it towards some recalcitrant log.

When the fire has entered the stage of embers, they need shifting around the sole. For this a rake is the implement. So is it when the time comes to remove them from the hearth. A wooden handled rake will serve, until it has been used too long among the flames. A metal implement from the garden centre will often have a plastic fixing, so is hopeless. The best is to have a rake head welded to a metal handle. If adaptation rules the day, a garden rake can be used with tines uppermost or facing down, but bakers' rakes, as Edlin mentions (below) were divided into two functions and forms. There was the rooker: more properly a single steel lath that turned a right-angle at the end of a pole to form a short-tailed L, and then a hoe-like instrument. In an Anglo-Saxon estate management handbook, there is reference to an *ofenraca*, and wooden rakes for this purpose of the period have been excavated in Sweden.

If the ash pit is an ash box, it will be necessary to lift the ash and cinders from the oven rather than merely let them fall. A shovel is required. The

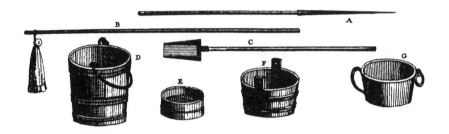

Figure 55: bakers' equipment from the same source as the previous illustrations. A is a peel, side elevation; B is a scuffle or mop; C is a shovel; D–G are buckets, measures and sieves.

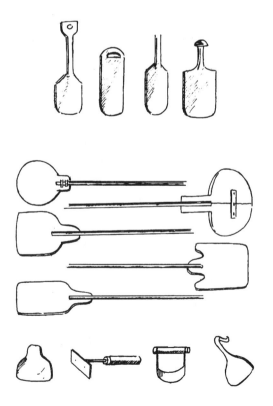

Figure 56: early breadmaking implements from Denmark, from an illustration in Hansen. The top row are dough cutters and spades for handling the dough in the trough. The centre group is a variety of oven peels. Below are some scrapers. Unlike in dairy work, scalding and washing of equipment was not an everyday habit in baking, especially as the seasoning of the wooden trough by months of successive sourdoughs made it more productive for the next batch. Gervase Markham explains how workmen's bread was leavened by being made in a seasoned trough in seventeenth-century England. Scrapers kept things clean, yet not so sterile as to kill the leavens and yeasts.

Figure 57: emblems of the baker's trade, from Randall Holmes, Academie of Armory, *1688. 1 is a meal shovel; 2 a dough trough; 3 a scraper; 4 a dough brake which was an aid to kneading – the lever is hinged at one end, the dough placed on the table and much pressure exerted on the handle of the lever; 5 a moulding table; 6 a knife; 7 an oven; 8 a bundle of furze and pitchfork; 9 a peel; and 10 a custard filler!*

baker's shovel in my possession has a flat, square blade, with a steel rod for a handle.

A rake does but a partial job of cleansing, which is finished with a scuffle. This is a pole or broom handle with a short chain nailed to one end. A more sophisticated arrangement is shown in figure 60. To this chain is tied a bundle of rags. The mobile mop is dipped in a bucket and introduced dripping into the oven. Amidst great clouds of steam you then swing it around in circles, swooshing out the ashes. This device will not only clean the oven, but can be used as a primitive form of temperature control. Repeated applications of the saturated scuffle will bring the heat down when the dough is pressing and the oven still too warm. However, in fact it will only reduce the heat of the sole, so the top crusts will probably burn anyway, though a way round that problem may be to bake with the door open – it is some mitigation. Pictures of scuffles and more simple mops, from Scappi onwards, occur in many illustrations (see figures 55, 58). According to the *Oxford English Dictionary*, the scuffle is a sort of hoe, and some use this word to describe the rake, not the mop. The correct word, though now obsolete, is malkin, mawkin or maukin. The dramatist Thomas Dekker refers to 'A beard filthier than a bakers maukin that he sweepes his oven.'

Failing this device, a saturated bristle sweeping brush can be employed. Have a bucket of water by the side of the oven, dip and sweep. Nylon brushes are not to be recommended, they melt. A brush will probably last only a short time. Live embers inevitably lodge amongst the bristles and wreak considerable havoc.

The scuffle may also be useful as a means of introducing moisture to the atmosphere, though often the steam it generates will have evaporated before the door is finally closed. It is a truism that crusts are crisper if steam is in the baking air, but most of the moisture comes from the loaves themselves, as the evaporation of water in the dough is not vented until the door is opened again. This is a principle cause of brick oven bread being better textured than domestic cooker bread. If more steam is wanted, a wet cloth can be be placed in the oven at the same time as the loaves are baked.

The writer A. Edlin, already referred to, includes notes on these and other instruments:

> *The rooker.* This is a long piece of iron, in shape somewhat resembling the letter L, fixed in a wooden handle. Its use is to draw out the ashes from all parts of the oven to the mouth.
>
> *The hoe.* This is a piece of iron, similar to a garden hoe, fixed in a handle, partly wood and partly iron. Its use is to scrape up such ashes and loose dust as escaped the rooker.
>
> *The swabber.* This is a common pole, about eight feet long, with a quantity of wet netting fastened to the end, Its use is to clean out the bottom of the oven, after the ashes have been removed, previous to setting in the bread.

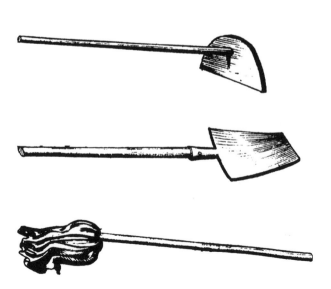

Figure 58: Italian instruments for the oven from Scappi, 1570: the mop, the rake and the shovel.

Figure 59: a detail from Bartolomeo Scappi, this time of one of his fire irons, which has the characteristic form of the baker's rooker.

The speed of firing is often a vexed question. The timetable sketched above is relaxed indeed. It does ensure that the heat builds up gradually, for absorption, rather than just a flash. It will therefore last as long as the insulation allows. If the oven is used infrequently, and has got damp, such a long, slow firing will be essential. When the structure is damp, the fire will not draw so well, and of course the materials take much longer to heat. But most accounts of firing small ovens, such as are found to the sides of domestic hearths for instance, imply that much less time is needed than I have posited. In part this is because an oven that is built inside the house, and which reposes at the side of an ever-burning kitchen fire, will be inherently warmer. It will also be a lot smaller, and the fire will be correspondingly more effective. The speed of firing could be improved by increasing the draught (that would mean introducing extra flues or in different locations, or expanding the door), and paying close attention to the type of wood burned.

The words of Eliza Acton, from her *English Bread Book*, though often cited, are instructive about firing ovens large and small:

Management of a brick oven. – Much of the quality of bread depends on its being well baked, and therefore, the nature and construction of the oven used for it, when it is required in large quantities, are very important. Of all that are in common use amongst us at present, a brick oven, heated with wood, is generally considered as the best adapted to it; and, certainly, no bread seems so sweet and wholesome as that which is so baked in private families, when perfect cleanliness has been observed in all the operations connected with it, and they have been performed with care and skill. To ensure a sufficient degree of heat to bake bread properly, and a variety of other things in succession after it when they are required, the oven should be well heated, then cleared and cleansed ready for use, and *closely shut* from half an hour to an hour, according to its size. It will not then cool down as it would if the baking were commenced immediately after the fire was withdrawn, but will serve for cakes, biscuits, sweet puddings, fruit, meat-jelly, jars of sago, tapioca, rice, and other preparations, for several hours after the bread is taken out.

I have known a very large brick oven, heated in the middle of the day with one full sized faggot or rather more, and a log or two of cord-wood, which was added when the faggot was partly consumed, still warm enough at eight or nine o'clock in the evening to bake various delicate small cakes, such as macaroons and *meringues*, and also custards, apples, &c.

It is both a great convenience and a considerable economy in many families to have such a means of preparing food for several days' consumption, and renders them entirely independent both of bakers and confectioners.

To restore the freshness of pastry, biscuits, or bread, when they begin to taste stale, it is only necessary to heat them through, without hardening them, in a gentle oven of any kind.

To heat a large brick oven. – Lay a quantity of shavings or other dry light fuel in the centre of the oven, and some small branches of faggot-wood upon them; over these place as many of the larger branches as will make a tolerably large fire, and set light to the shavings. As the wood consumes keep adding more, throwing in, after a time, amongst the live embers the stout poles of the faggot, and, lastly, two or three moderate-sized logs of cord-wood, when the oven is of large dimensions and the heat is wanted to be long-sustained. When no cord-wood is at hand, the necessary quantity of large faggot or other wood must be used instead.

From an hour and a half to two hours will be required to heat thoroughly a full-sized brick oven. The fire should be spread over it in all parts towards the end of the time, that the whole of the floor may be in a proper state for baking.

After all the embers and ashes have been cleared out, a large mop, kept exclusively for the purpose, dipped into hot water and wrung very dry, should be passed in every direction over it, to cleanse it perfectly for the reception of the bread.

As the heat is greatest at the further part of the oven (and at the *sides* frequently), it is usual to place loaves of the largest size there, and those which require less baking nearer to the mouth of the oven.

To ascertain whether a brick oven be heated to the proper degree for baking bread, it is customary for persons who have not much experience to throw a small quantity of flour into it. Should it take fire immediately, or become black, the oven is too hot, and should be closed, if the state of the dough will permit it to wait, until the temperature is moderated: this is better than cooling it down quickly by leaving the door open. It may also be tested by putting into it small bits of dough about the size of walnuts, which will soon show whether it be over heated or not sufficiently so.

When, from want of due calculation or any other point of good management, the dough is not ready when the oven is fit to receive it, and the heat has too much abated by the time it is so to permit it to be properly baked, the economist should bear in mind *that the cost of having it heated anew to the proper degree will be a very trifling consideration compared with the loss of the bread itself, if it should be spoiled by insufficient baking.* The price of half a bushel of flour would purchase a *large* number of faggots.

Cottage brick oven

To bake half a bushel of bread in the oven of a working man's cottage, a *fourpenny faggot* – in those counties where wood is to be obtained at a reasonable price – is usually found sufficient. The bread in many cases is divided into eight or nine large loaves, which are baked for about two hours. The fire is kindled in the oven immediately after the dough is made; but it is not commonly left to rise so long as two hours, much more yeast being used for it oftener than is really needed, and the fermentation being much quickened in consequence.

The temperatures for baking and cooking in brick ovens are the same as in conventional domestic machines, but the nature of the heat will mean that cooking times are reduced. With the ceiling height specified, 450°F is the highest safe temperature for cooking bread without burning the crust. Earlier writers are often insistent on the height of the vault being between 20 and 24 inches (500–600mm) so as to maximise the effect of radiant heat. The heat of a brick oven is more penetrating than a tin box heated by gas. There is radiation from the ceiling and walls, there is contact with the thoroughly heated sole, and there is the air itself, unable to escape by any vent. A kilo loaf, therefore, might cook in 20 minutes or even less, a pizza in five minutes, and a batch of tin loaves will also be well cooked in 20–25 minutes, even though ranged close to each other in a row.

Heating the oven can often be an approximate business. There is no exact way, for example, of telling the heat achieved before extinguishing the fire. The telltales mentioned by Eliza Acton – the sprinkling of flour, tiny dough balls – operate once the oven is prepared. What happens if they tell you it is too cool? Today, a thermometer is the simple test, once the ash is removed. Although it would be possible to instal probes and devices in the middle of the fabric to give instant information of heat absorption, during the firing, the best indicator is the state of the roof. While the burn is in its first stages, smoke blackens the bricks. As the heat builds up and the fire clears, so the roof begins to glow and appears completely clean. Once all the roof is clear, there is probably sufficient heat. As the fire dies to embers, if the burn has been successful, there is a comforting roar as the exhaust rushes through the doorway.

The rubbish out of the way, failing a thermometer, one can always test by hand. If you can hold your bare hand in the middle of the oven for more than a few seconds, it is too cool. If the oven is used daily, routine and familiarity are good substitutes for mechanical measures, but it is sobering how quickly the memory fades if use is more spasmodic.

The household recipe book of the English diarist and virtuoso John Evelyn, dating from the second half of the seventeenth century, contains many references to the brick oven and its use for different cooking processes. In several, the temperature of the oven, although described by analogy, is plainly critical. For example,

> Banbury Cake. ...set all in the oven till it be done, the oven being heated as for manchetts.
>
> The Lady Harrington's cake. ...bake it in the oven heated up as for manchetts, if it browne overmuch spread a paper on it; a cake of a peck may stand in the oven two hours.
>
> A Spanish foole. ...bake it in a dish, or paste, like a pie, as you please, then strew some carrawayes upon it, but have a care the oven be not too hott.
>
> To bake venison or beefe to keep all the yeare. ...put it into the oven it being as hott as for venison letting it stand in the oven an hower longer than you would a pasty of venison.
>
> Curranscakes. ...the oven must not be much hotter then it is after the drawing a good batch of bread.

To make Taffata tarts. …bake them in a temperate oven, which you must trie by throwing flowre into the oven, and if the flowre sparkle, it is too hott, if it only browne then sett in your tarts, which must stay in the oven till they have done boiling and be sure the oven lid be not sett up.

To make ice and snow in the ice. …set it in an oven after manchet is drawn.

To collar beef. …past[e] it [the pot] over with coarse dough, put it into the oven with household bread and let it stand all night. When you draw it out of the the oven the next morning take it out of the pott as hott as you can without breaking it.

Cake. …it will require two hours baking and the oven stop[p]ed after the scorching is over, and a sheet or two of paper as you see occasion dried and layed on the top of the cake to keepe it from too much coloring.

One of the most succinct, yet instructive, accounts of cooking in a wood-fired oven is that written by William Ellis, already referred to.

By this time I will suppose your oven to be in a forwardness of heating, by one that tends and looks after the fire, while you are cutting and moulding the dough into the form of half peck or peck loaves, that as they are made should be lain on a linen cloth, or on a board well flower'd, at a little distance from each other, to prevent their touching and sticking. Next examine your oven's heat. If on rubbing a stick the sparks of it fly briskly about, it is enough; then sweep it clean, and rub the bottom of the oven with a broom first, and presently after with a wet mop, or what the bakers call a maukin; then if it is over-hot, shut up the oven's mouth, lest it scorch the bread too much, and make it harsh; after this set in your loaves as fast as you can, placing the largest at the further end and round the sides, and the rest in the middle. It should also be observed, that in heating an oven, the dead coals or ashes of wood, furze, fern, straw, or other fewel, should be taken now and then out with the peel and thrown away, because these rather check than increase the heat. Care likewise should be used to burn the fewel in all places alike, by firing it sometimes on one side and sometimes on the other; which done, stop the mouth of the oven close. If it is an iron-plated door, wet rags are sufficient, and so they will be to a wooden stopper if it shuts very close, else we lay wet rags first and dirt over them. Three hours time is enough to bake a batch of half-peck loaves; if peck loaves, four or five hours must be allowed, and when the time is expired, draw your bread; and if you find one or more loaves not baked enough, put them in again, stop up, and let them remain longer, but not too long, lest it give the bread a brown colour and an ill taste.

It is difficult sometimes to square the accounts of baking bread in early cookery books and other literature with present-day experience. It seems, to us, that baking times were unacceptably long; and that important phases in the preparation of dough are occasionally omitted from recipes. The bread recipes from a not-very-distinguished, anonymous, cookery book dating from around 1833, *The New Female Instructor; or, Young Woman's Guide to Domestic Happiness* may serve by way of illustration. Recipes and text have strong resonances from Mrs Rundell's earlier book, as well as J.A. Stewart's *The young woman's companion* of 1814 (see Dena Attar, *A Bibliography of Household Books Published in Britain 1800–1914*).

Its comments on flour were echoes of many others. American flour, it observed, was more economic than softer British flour, as it absorbed up to twice as much water. A stone (14 lb, 6.3 kg) of American flour makes 21.5 lb (9.75 kg) of bread, while English flour only makes 18.5 lb (8.5 kg). Interestingly, the measure still holds good for flour 150 years later. A batch of yeasted bread made according to the common household recipe of 1.75 lb (785 g) flour to 15 fluid ounces (450 ml) of water will result in 21.5 lb (9.7 kg) of dough. In fact, a 'strong' bread flour bought at the grocer's, whether of European or North American origin, will probably absorb at least 18 fluid ounces (540 ml) of water for a straight dough made by hand, but the *Instructor*'s note regarding English flour is perhaps a measure of how soft it was in the 1830s – making heavy, slightly risen loaves. The Fortescue family of north Devon were bringing in American flour in the 1840s in order to bake the finer bread and rolls required for the family table, leaving the home-grown wheatmeal for the servants.

The *Instructor*'s household bread entailed the oven be lit at the same time as the main dough was kneaded in the trough – having first made a sponge or starter to give it rapid progress,

> by the time it [the oven] is warm enough, the dough will be ready. Make the loaves about five pounds each; sweep out the oven very clean and quick, and put in the bread; shut it up close, and two hours and a half will bake it. ... If baked in tins, the crust will be very nice.
>
> The oven should be round, not long, and the roof from twenty to twenty-four inches high, the mouth small, and the door of iron, to shut close. This construction will save firing and time, and bake better than long and high-roofed ovens. [This is a standard recommendation, met in many nineteenth-century cookery books.]

In the recipe for 'The Rev. Mr. Hagget's economical Bread' (found in Mrs Rundell), the *Instructor* remarks that the rather heavy loaf, made with a wholemeal flour from which the coarsest bran has been sieved – used in turn to make an infusion of bran-water as liquor for the dough - would last long enough so that, 'when ten days old, if put in the oven for twenty minutes, [it] will appear quite new again.'

The recipe for 'French Bread', as in most English books, is enriched with eggs and milk, worked into 'a thin and light dough. Stir it about, but do not knead it. Have ready three quart wooden dishes, divide the dough among them, set to rise, then turn them out into the oven which must be quick. Rasp when done.'

The three loaves were made from a dough of 3.5 lb (1.6 kg) of white flour, three eggs and a pint of liquor. By modern standards, the flour must have been weak indeed to make a slack dough with this amount of liquid. Equally, the gluten was barely woken by the residual kneading that was counselled. Instead, the dough was moulded straight away into the wooden bowls serving as *bannetons* or proving baskets. Once risen, it was baked. The oven being so hot, the crust was best removed by a rasp, or chipped off with a knife (the preferred way for John Farley, the London cook, who claimed a knife left the loaf a better colour, presumably because it was not so even or effective).

English taste was not enamoured of crusts - one presumes it was taste, not teeth. From earliest records, a bread rasp was essential kitchen equipment. The historian Ann Hagen, writing of Anglo-Saxon bread reminds us that loaves were illustrated crustless, with their sides cut off. In the household account for 1417 of Robert Waterton of Methley, near Leeds, a gaoler of Richard II when he was in Pontefract Castle, there is an item, 'spent on one *myursene* bought this year, 2d.', the word deriving from the verb 'to mye', i.e. to grate or crumb (French *mie* = crumb) bread. The instrument was doubtless as much for preparing crumbs for thickened sauces as for rasping crusts.

The use of the rasp was perhaps determined by two or three facts. The first was that fresh bread was not the *sine qua non* it is today. Medieval bakers of London were not permitted to sell from their houses or workshops – rather the bread was sold in public markets (to guard against cheats) held on two days a week. No fresh bread there. The Restoration woman cookery writer Hannah Woolley advises that 'it is a point of ill Huswifery to eat hot or very new Bread' . The Victorian doctor Pye Henry Chavasse, in his *Advice to Mothers on the Management of their Offspring* (1839), counselled against new and heavy bread, two or three days old was better, for the proper regulation of children's digestion; advice echoed down the years – at least until my schooldays. Furthermore, most loaves were of a size impossible to consume in a day. The great loaves eaten in farmhouses, often of maslin – rye and wheat mixed – might weigh a stone or more. In nineteenth-century Denmark, a large farming household would make rye loaves weighing 10–12 kg. The average weekly consumption of bread among working men in Northumberland in 1863 was computed at 15 lb (6.75 kg). This was probably bought from the baker as quartern loaves, made from 3.5 lb (1500 g) of flour. They lasted, as did the Rev. Mr. Hagget's, for a week at least. At the north Devon house of Castle Hill, the seat of the Fortescue family, a baker came in once a week to bake the household loaves. Even today some bread is better for sitting. Rye breads, particularly, are almost impossible to cut in the first hours after baking – the knife clogs its teeth, and the crumb collapses under the strain. Whole styles of baking were devoted to long life: the pumpernickel is a bread for eating the winter through; the Scandinavian dried rye breads were designed with the same end in view. Modern French breads, when based on *levain* (leaven) not *levure* (yeast), are happy to last five days.

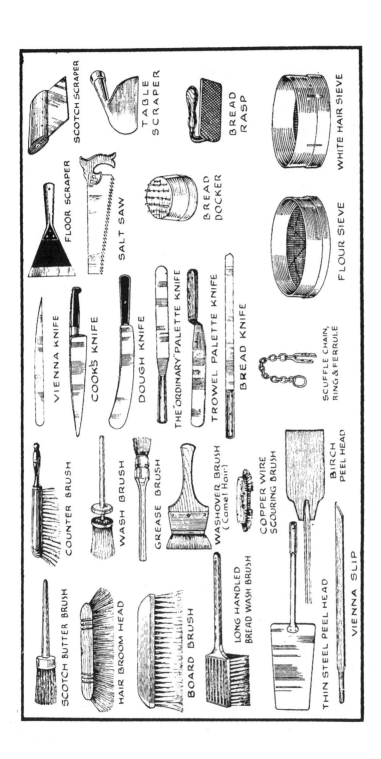

Figure 60: a plate from Walter Banfield's excellent commercial bakery manual, Manna, depicting the various instruments of the bakehouse as used in 1937. A bread rasp is shown centre-right. The docker is for makingholes in the top of loaves before they go into the oven, depicted in prints from the seventeenth century. The two scrapers ('Scotch' and 'table') are near identical to those shown in the French print, figure 54. The scuffle chain is shown centre bottom.

Having said that, there are many instances of fresh bread being preferred: Gillian Goodwin cites the rules of the medieval household of Duke Humphrey of Gloucester, where the duke had today's, the members of the upper household yesterday's, and brown bread for the rest was served at three days old. The *Ménagier de Paris*, at the same time, advises his pupil-wife that when a wedding feast is arranged, flat white loaves baked the day before should be ordered, and trencher bread should be four days old.

These loaves, to take an eighteenth-century recipe from the manuscripts of the Yorkshire mansion Castle Howard as example, were baked for five hours. And baking time is the second fact with reference to rasps. Early breads, cooked in wood-fired ovens, were either quickly cooked, like the manchet loaves, in a very hot oven (recall Evelyn's recipe book, noted above), or took an unconsciable time, and were usually pretty large. Looking at the flour accounts for the Fortescues in nineteenth-century Devon, week after week the average weight of flour per loaf is 3.5 lb (1500 g). It is clear that several sorts of bread were baked, doubtless of differing sizes. Therefore we may assume the common household bread weighed quite a lot more than the average, while the finer white bread for the family table was in smaller loaves – sixteenth-century manchets, for instance, weighed about 8 ounces (225 g) according to William Harrison. (Not all early loaves were gigantic. The French historian Françoise Desportes has calculated from several different sources that the medieval French town loaf ranged from 350 g to 500 g – not far from our own range today.)

Large loaves in an oven for hours on end might indicate two things: that the ovens were not overheated, otherwise the crusts would burn to a cinder; and that the crusts would none the less be tremendously thick and progressively tough as the week passed. Remember the loaves would be stored in the open air, high in the kitchen on a bread 'grate' (so called in some sixteenth century inventories) or 'car' (a giant of the form may be seen at the Welsh Folk Museum at St Fagan's, near Cardiff, along with a reconstructed wood-fired communal oven) : a lattice grid that hung from the ceiling, high above the well-worn routes of nocturnal rodents. Small wonder that some would rasp off the crusts before eating, just as they would grate the manchet crusts, which were done in a hot oven and thus often burned and blackened.

Another remedy of impossible crusts was taking the bread as soon as it came out of the oven and, rather than cooling on racks as we do today, wrapping it in flannel cloths. This would soften the crust, if nothing else.

The coolness of the ovens when prepared for household bread helps explain, for me, the common omission from early bread recipes of any final proof. Lady Clark of Tillypronie recommends that ovens for all breadmaking should be 'of moderate heat'. Although the recipe for French bread given by the *Instructor* proves in wooden bowls before baking, his household bread is simply moulded then baked. If the oven were cool enough, there would be a fair oven 'spring' to give lightness to the dough, for the working of the yeast would not be killed by too great a temperature. That this lack of final proof was often intended may be inferred from a succeeding recipe in the *Instructor*, for 'Brentford Rolls' (also from Mrs Rundell).

> Mix with two pounds of flour, a little salt, two ounces of sifted sugar, four ounces of butter, and two eggs beaten with two spoonfuls of yeast, and about a pint of milk. Knead the dough well, and set it to rise before the fire. Make twelve rolls, butter tin plates, and set them before the fire to rise, till they become of a proper size; then bake half an hour.

If writers can mention proving in one place, their lack of reference to it in others must be intentional. This may be confirmed by study of Eliza Acton, perhaps the most detailed early English bread book, where some doughs are given a second rise in the trough or crock, others a final proof in the tin or bowl, and some just a single bulk fermentation. Note, however, that William Ellis, in the quotation above, does envisage a final proof.

The recipe book of Lady Clark of Tillypronie is interesting. Several of her entries advise a final proof, indeed rather an overproof such as her Birk Hall bread that should have 'eaves' hanging over the sides of the tin when ready for the oven, but her oven-bottom bread is put straight in the oven after knocking back from the first rise. Her brown bread recipe ends with a note that when the dough is sufficiently spongy, it be divided into loaves and baked immediately, unless a light porous loaf is required, when the dough should prove in the tins for half an hour.

The *Instructor* states that bread baked in tins will have a 'nice' crust. By this, he means tender. The English were not the only people to bake in tins, but the preference does seem more often encountered in northern than in southern Europe: the Scots, for example, were masters of the art. The French call their tin-bread *pain de mie*. Apart from the desire for a soft crust, there are at least two other factors that could have had an influence. Tin-bread packs more tightly into an oven, is therefore more economical. Tins contain a highly yeasted, high-rising dough with more facility. Given our fondness for tins antedates the mechanical toaster or the sandwich lunch, convenience of shape cannot have had the consequences it has in these days of sliced white.

The fire has burned, is raked and scuffled, the temperature established. All that needs be done is the bread charged, either in tins, or directly on the sole. For this you need a peel (figures 56 and 61, and others). The word derives from the Latin *pala*, and the French *pelle*: a spade or shovel. Peels vary in shape and size, as well as material, depending on the loaf or object to be inserted or withdrawn. Broad round peels are needed for large round loaves, long thin ones for baguettes or Vienna breads. If your peel is too large for the job, it will probably damage loaves already placed in the oven; if too small, the trembling dough will teeter off the edge as you turn it out of the proving basket and slash it with the necessary cuts.

Peels are as necessary for placing tins as for loaves that are baked on the floor of the oven. But you may prefer a blade of metal that slides under the tin with greater ease.

Metal peels can be purchased at dealers who supply the bakery and pizza trades. Wooden peels can be made at home. A slip peel for baguettes can be cut out of a 150mm plank, then planed and sanded to give thin edges. A round peel is best made of a piece of plywood cut to shape and sanded round the edges, then fixed to a broom handle.

The enormous peels that can be seen in serious bakeries are a reflection of the great depth of the oven. There is considerable skill in manipulating the blade of such an instrument when it is at the end of a five-metre handle.

Getting the loaves off the peel is a knack quickly learned. Ensure there is some flour or other lubricant on the blade – no greater tragedy than losing the loaf at the last moment as the sticky dough resolutely sticks to the peel. Bakers use finely ground rice, called 'cones', as the dusting material of last resort: it has no gluten, is pure starch, and will not affect the consistency of the dough. Turn the loaf from the proving basket so as to present the right side upwards. Cut the loaf with your blade. Insert the peel into the oven and, as it gets to the chosen spot, give it a rapid, but not too violent, push-pull movement to eject the loaf gently on to the floor. If too vigorous, the loaf can shoot off and hit the wall, or a previously deposited loaf. If too tentative, or should the blade not allow free movement, half the loaf will be on the oven floor, the rest still stretched on the peel.

A final essential, for night baking, is illumination so the farthest corner of the oven can be seen. Early bakers would leave a small fire in the front so that light was given by flickering flame. Modern commercial ovens have insulated lighting devices. The home baker will probably be content with a torch – even a lamp worn on the head currently de rigueur for cavers or night-time sports enthusiasts (good for reading books in tents, too).

Figure 61: some English oven peels. Those below are from the north of England and are drawn by Peter Brears.

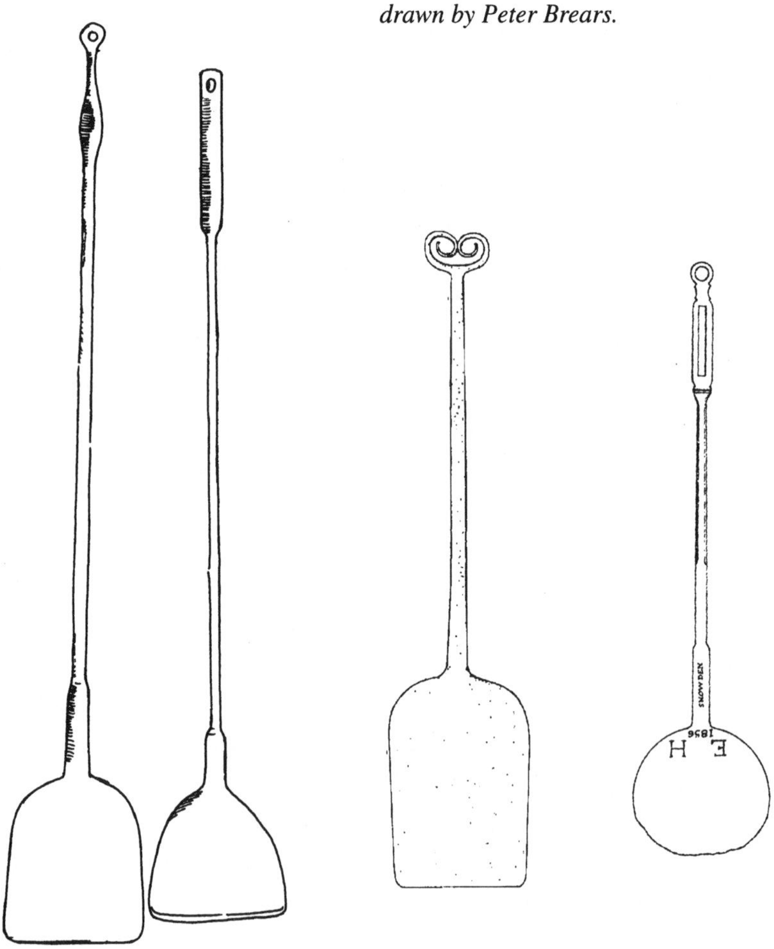

RESTORATION

Whereas earlier sections have discussed building from scratch, many people already have an oven in their house which could be revitalised and restored.

Not everyone, however. Hearth may be a synonym for house, but an oven was a specific tool either beyond the financial reach of many householders, impractical because of their situation – living hugger-mugger in cities with neighbours – or simply not part of their culinary world view – such as those living on the fringes of Europe, beyond the wheaten zone, who relied rather on fire and bakestone.

Scotland was just such a society. Wheat was grown in the more temperate districts, and wheaten bread baked and eaten in a few large cities or grand mansions, but the majority ate oats or berecorn until well into the last century. By 1812 in the highlands, there were only two bakers, at Thurso and Wick, importing flour for wheaten bread. At Wigtown in the south west, there was one baker in 1755, and four or five at the end of the century. Thus brick ovens, ripe for restoration, are here a rarity.

In Finland, as a more distant example, although there were ovens in private houses in the south-eastern province of Karelia, those who lived in the west depended on large communal ovens that were fired infrequently. 'The baking of bread for the summer was done in the spring as long as there was snow on the shingle roofs. The next time the oven was heated was after harvesting, when new flour was available.'

Any society that consumed bread in large quantity had to cook it somewhere. This meant one of three locations: at home; in a communal oven shared between several households; or in a commercial baker's shop.

That all Europeans who lived in pre-industrial times baked their own bread at home is a myth. It is speedily dispelled by reading two English authors of the last century, William Cobbett and Eliza Acton. Both regretted the decline in home breadmaking, and indeed wrote books encouraging its re-adoption. Both also observed that home baking was more prevalent in the north than the south of the country, and a simple correlation between economic development and self-reliance must be drawn. Since the rise of settled urban cultures in ancient Egypt, Greece and Rome, the transfer of responsibility for bread production from individual household to professional cadre as society became more concentrated and sociologically more complicated has appeared inevitable. In Anglo-Norman Winchester, Baldwin the baker was a citizen of substance, renting a number of properties, and there were at least five other bakers in the town. Bread is a commodity that responds well to being produced in bulk; bread ovens are capital-intensive. The conclusion is plain.

Where professional bakers were active, bread ovens were likely to be concentrated on their premises, and thus not available for modern restoration. Indeed, medieval urban regulations, for instance in the city of London, actually inhibited the building of private ovens for fear of fire and its consequences. This said, it is clear from probate inventories, for instance some from Exeter in the sixteenth and seventeenth centuries, that some merchants' houses – of the more substantial classes – did have their own bakehouses.

In medieval Europe, as has been explained in great detail by Louis Stouff in his study of food supplies in Provence, there arose a distinction between those who ran the ovens and those who made the dough and this is introduction enough to the whole concept of the communal oven: a single building serving several households. Figure 68 is a particularly glorious example of one of these, in the small French town of Urval in the Dordogne.

Such community ventures existed in many places: Finland has been mentioned, the Swiss Valais, industrial towns in northern England, the province of Quebec in Canada, and so on. Some of them, perhaps the more elaborate, were the day-to-day responsibility of a *fornarius* or oven-master, who contracted to bake those loaves brought to him for a set fee. Later on, such a relationship subsisted between commercial bakers (once the callings of oven-master and baker had been combined) and neighbouring households, whether it was for the baking of bread, finishing the Sunday roast, or producing Samuel Pepys's favourite venison pasties. The book by the Swedish photographer Kerstin Bernhard of evocative studies of Greek bakers handling loaves from a queue of housewives is eloquent testimony of this arrangement in recent times.

Individual ovens existed more often in isolated rural dwellings where there were insufficient neighbours to form a cooperative, or a population large enough to support a professional baker. Or they were found in the houses of the well-to-do who preferred to supply themselves to their own specification. That the enthusiasms of the householder informed the activities in the kitchen is a truism, but an exchange of letters between Sir Ralph Verney of Claydon in Buckinghamshire and his steward during the Commonwealth does under-line it. The royalist Sir Ralph was contemplating a return to England out of France in 1653 and his thoughts turned to cooks and employing Besse Heath and her husband, though he could not be much use to the family 'at London (for there wants neither Bakers nor Brewers)', sign enough of the man's role in the partnership, and the lack of private ovens in urban situations. In the event, another was employed, recruited in London and dispatched to the country where Sir Ralph is afraid that 'idlenesse may spoyle him,' so encourages the steward to set him to learning to read and write and 'baking French bread in the great Brasse Baking Pans.' At the same time, a French servant who was with Sir Ralph in Brussels has been sent to Blois to learn how to make pastry and good French bread, and the baronet is minutely concerned to make sure of supplies of good white flour at Claydon to carry on the production.

Some plans of English houses with ovens are shown in figure 62. These are substantial examples, where the oven occupies its own space: constitutes in fact a bakehouse. Survivals such as these are not common; nor, in England, are free-standing ovens such as are often found in Mediterranean countries where a more settled climate encourages the pursuit of open-air bakery.

The most common form of brick or masonry oven surviving today is one that shares the chimney of the main kitchen fire so that there was no need to construct separate ventilation. Within a great hearth, the oven, occasionally more than one, could be tucked to one side. Its insulation consisted of the mass of the principal chimney, already warmed and dried by the constant flame of the kitchen. Removal of the spent fuel was trouble-free, smoke went straight up the chimney. Nothing could be simpler. Invariably, these ovens have been superseded by cast iron ranges in the nineteenth century, or electric or gas cookers in our own time, however, a country priest in west Devon in 1922 recorded that on his rounds of the parish one afternoon he called at six houses, and five of them were still using their cloam ovens for baking bread.

Some old hearth arrangements appear to have a main oven and a smaller cupboard close to it. This aumbry was the resting place of the piece of dough held back to act as the starter for the next baking day. An item in a Devon antiquarian collection of 1925 records, with not much corroboration, that Exeter bakers used to make balls of flour and water paste and wrap them round a piece of fat. The lump was put in this proving cupboard for seven days when it would have started a lactic fermentation for a sourdough leaven.

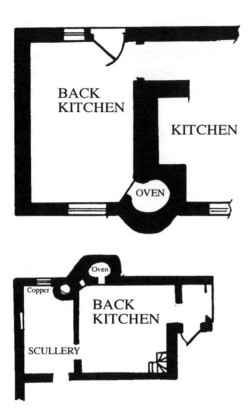

Figure 62: plans of ovens in existing English farmhouses. Only the one at the bottom has the oven in the main kitchen, the others confining it to the back kitchen or bakehouse.

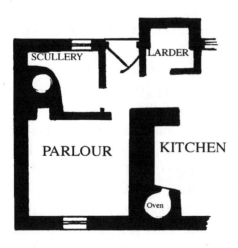

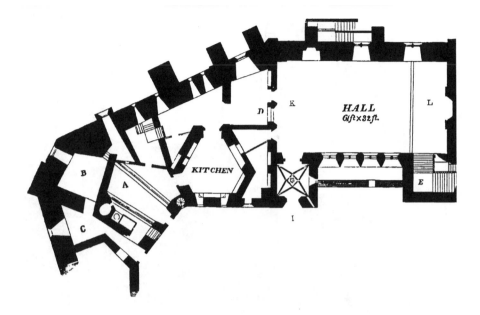

Figure 63: plan of the domestic offices at Berkeley Castle, Gloucestershire where the installation is altogether grander than the everyday farmhouse. At the screens end of the great hall, marked K, there were three doors, one leading to the buttery, one to the pantry and the centre opening (D) to the kitchen. The bakehouse, converted to a scullery in later years, is marked A. B was the larder, and C the dairy.

The placing of the oven in relation to the hearth is not particularly significant, but some have noticed they are often placed opposite the window or source of light so that the loaves can be placed inside without collision.

Richard Bacon, whose book on ovens in New England has already been referred to, describes many domestic installations that were next to, rather than in, the kitchen hearth, and were vented independently. Such an oven is illustrated in figure 64. The square exterior belies its arched roof within, making is somewhat akin to the great square ovens that developed alongside the eastern European and Russian stove. Beneath these independent ovens was often an ash pit. The form is not so common in Britain.

Restoration of an existing oven should be taken in two stages. First its emplacement and viability should be assessed, then one may turn to the detail of its construction and condition.

Figure 64: a drawing of a farmhouse kitchen in Virginia that shows an oven in the same room as the kitchen hearth, but vented independently. The oven flue, which joins the main flue higher up, is set behind the door to the oven so that it was possible to burn a fire on the sole with the door shut, or at least with only enough open to provide a draught. The smoke should not then leak into the room itself. The space below was an ash pit.

We are no longer prepared to accept rooms full of smoke such as might have been a medieval, or indeed an eighteenth-century kitchen. Any oven, therefore, must be capable of venting to a satisfactory flue, and provided with sufficient draught that the smoke will go up, not out into the room itself. When the oven is sited next to the main kitchen hearth, this is not a problem – unless the flue has been blocked or diminished, or devoted to serving a single appliance such as woodburning stove, Rayburn or Aga. In this case, consideration will have to be given to breaking into the existing flue at a higher point, or building a new chimney.

Whenever a new chimney is built, fireproofing is paramount, and a good draught comes next. This is not a builder's handbook, so I can only recommend application to a competent builder – I hesitate to say architect – as well as consultation with the manufacturers of any appliance that is

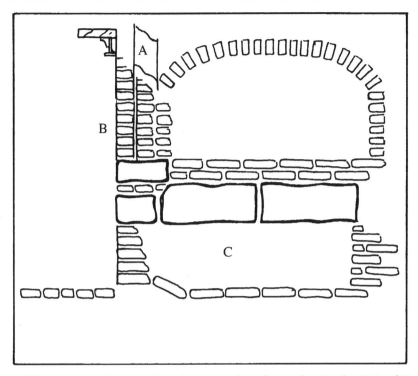

Figure 65: a cross-section of an American oven, based on a drawing by Richard Bacon. The oven itself sits on a platform of granite slabs, above the ash pit (C), which is sunk slightly below ground level. This, like the oven on the preceding page, is vented (A) behind its door (B), and breaks into the main kitchen flue at a higher level. The oven is 537mm high, the ash pit 337mm, and the oven door 337mm.

'plumbed into' any flue you may be thinking of invading in case such an act vitiates the functioning of the chimney as designed. With fire precautions in mind, statutory building regulations may also come into play.

If a new flue is contemplated, it would necessarily have to be external to the oven, unless you were to change the original shape of the installation. A cowl would have to be constructed, ensuring that it is capacious enough to swallow the smoke as it emerges from the oven's mouth. Were your oven like that from Skipton illustrated in figure 66, or one of the New England types such as in figure 65, with a built-in flue, it is possible, even probable, that the chimney survives to serve the arrangement. All that needs be done is to check it works, and have it cleaned.

Ovens that vent directly into a functioning kitchen fireplace are simpler to manage, provided you avoid stepping into the blazing hearth as you tend the

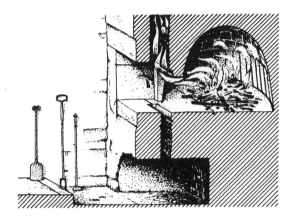

Figure 66: a cut-away view of an oven at Skipton Castle, drawn by Peter Brears. The flue is behind the main opening, and there is a slot for the ash to be raked into the pit without spreading filth and glowing coals into the kitchen as a whole. A small rake, a shovel and oven fork are depicted standing at the ready.

loaves, inasmuch as there is an immediate location for the spent embers and ashes when the oven is raked. Of all the phases in preparing an oven for baking, raking is the messiest and most fraught with danger. No houseproud spirit will accept half an inch of ash over shining copper; no fire brigade will understand the excuses.

Ovens of the New England type, therefore, require careful management if they are not to cause trouble. In my own life, it is a common occurrence to rake out a half-burnt fire: I miscalculate the firing time, I get too excited in charging with wood, the dough suddenly takes off and I need the oven now, not some time in the relaxed future. This will not be possible with an indoor oven that is not actually sited within the fireplace. Firing, therefore, will need to be a precise matter. Experience will be necessary to gauge exactly how much wood to use, and probably of what sort, to achieve a set temperature so that it may burn out completely, making the raking a less hazardous task.

Even if this ideal position is reached, it will be necessary to have a foolproof and sophisticated system of catching the ashes in a metal box with a tight-fitting lid so that sparks are quickly extinguished.

The oven with an internal flue raises another question not yet addressed: dampers or shutters to close the chimney at the end of firing and during baking. When the flue is outside the oven chamber itself, the door acts as a damper, that is, it stops the escape of heat up the open chimney. If, however, it is vented the far side of the door, the flue must be capable of closure. If the oven has not been used for decades, any metal fitment will have perished or rusted too much to be revived. Early dampers are usually simple sliding plates and easily replaced.

If the oven is not large, the door will occupy proportionately more of its surface. The greater the area relative to the volume of the oven, the more important is efficient and complete closure to avoid too rapid an escape of heat and decline in baking temperature. When loaves are cooked for an hour or more, a tight seal is still more necessary; small wonder the opening used to be stopped with a line of clay or dough round the edge of the door. It made inspection halfway through cooking an impossibility.

The door is the single part of an existing oven most likely to have dissolved from senescence. If the masonry was fashioned to permit the installation of a hinged door with catch that can be created by a blacksmith or metalworking shop, so much the better. Otherwise, any self-supporting door of the sort mentioned in respect of the Prospect oven can be used.

When the moving parts of the oven have been identified and planned for, then is the time to look at the fabric: the brick and stone work, the floor and the mortar. Where the brick or stone arch and walls are concerned, if they are not in collapse – in which case nothing short of dismantling and reconstruction is possible – it is the mortar that is most often in need of attention. Repointing will be tiresome and uncomfortable, but pay good dividends. Just as was counselled with the Prospect oven, mortar should not be too strong – it should have elasticity and not be stronger than the materials it is jointing. An informed builder may be able to advise the mixing of a mortar that corresponds closely with the original, but if in doubt, something as limey as possible is to be recommended. Rake the joints out deeply, keep the fabric moist so as not to lose all the goodness in the first application of the trowel, and to attain maximum adhesion.

The floor may have worn too much to make repair a simple matter. If oven-bottom breads are contemplated, then smoothness is essential. Perhaps a screed may be laid over the existing surface using fire cement as an expensive but easily obtainable material. Or the bricks or slab forming the sole can be excavated and replaced in all the important areas by new work laid on a cement base with sand spread over in the same fashion as already described with the new oven. This should not be an impossible task, and the principles adumbrated with new work hold good with restoration.

If the emplacement of the original oven is satisfactory, giving good venting, convenient for work, and so on, but the fabric is completely incapable of restoration, three alternatives present themselves. The oven embrasure can be excavated and a facsimile recreated. Or the hole can be filled with a modern version of a cloam oven bought from a manufacturer of terracotta ovens. Or you can embark on constructing your own cement or clay lined shell in the space available. Whichever course is chosen, the emplacement of an indoor oven is the really important thing to get right. The risks of fire are too great to jest about; the distress caused by the mess may result in who-knows-what ructions and disagreements. With a garden oven, the baker is able to play happily at his preoccupation without inconveniencing others.

Figure 67: a detail from a French print of the eighteenth century. The beehive oven here depicted seems to have the fire under the oven sole, not on it. Compare the oven in the print on the title page, which has the same arrangement. These were called Jewish ovens, and the type is known in the middle east (see page 12), though I have never myself seen one in Europe.

Figure 68: the communal oven at Urval in the Dordogne. The giant peel can be seen rest-ing at the bottom of the staging above the oven mouth -– which presumably was installed as a place to house loaves waiting for oven space.

RECIPE

Although this is not cookery book, and it is unlikely that readers will embark on building an oven without some enthusiasm for and knowledge of baking in conventional appliances, I give the simplest of recipes to act as stimulus to those who need further encouragement.

Historians record with wonder the vast number of sorts of bread available to the ancient Egyptians, or the Greeks, or the Romans, and today a selling point of many cooks and bakers is that they concoct an infinite variety of recipes to please every mood and palate. For my part, I have found the hunt for novelty intriguing and unnecessary. Bread comes in two or three types, and that is enough for most to explore the immeasurable quirks and characteristics of flour, water, salt and leavening.

If variety is the spice of your crust, many books will give counsel. I mention those by Elizabeth David, Carol Field and Joe Ortiz in particular. I have been very struck by a long recipe for naturally leavened bread written by Nancy Silverton if you enjoy minute instruction. A survey of several types of breads, including many sorts of fermentations, is contained in my *Making Bread at Home*.

HOUSEHOLD BREAD

This recipe is a simple extension of the plainest yeasted bread. By giving it time in fermentation, some development of flavour is allowed. Many sorts of flour, and mixes, can be used, each having their own effect.

400 g bread flour
225–275 ml water
15 g fresh yeast

Make a dough of these ingredients. The amount of water will depend on the flour used. The dough should be neither too firm nor too slack. Leave to rise in a bowl at room temperature. Because all the rises in this recipe are slow, the doughs will skin during their times of fermentation unless they are well covered with oiled film. When this dough has doubled in size, knock back and place in a plastic bag in the refrigerator. Leave it for 24–36 hours. The next day, withdraw it and make a second dough.

225–275 ml hand-hot water
the dough from the first day
400 g bread flour

Break the dough into the water, add the flour and knead well to excite the gluten. Leave to rise under oiled film for about three hours, until doubled in size, in a well-warmed room, about 75°F.

850–900 ml hand-hot water
the second-stage dough
15 g fresh yeast
1.5 kg bread flour
50 g salt

Repeat the procedure outlined for the second stage. Leave to rise for around three hours until doubled in size. The addition of the extra yeast should ensure that the dough and the oven are synchronised. It may be omitted if a more relaxed timetable can be contemplated.

When fermentation is complete, divide into five 600 g loaves, retaining the remainder of the dough in a plastic bag in the refrigerator for the next baking day. It will last in cold store for 3–5 days without a thought. It will not take many bakes to develop a certain sourness of flavour. However, that sourness will get too strong if the bulk fermentation is allowed to be too slow.

Prove the loaves in baskets, covering them to guard against skinning. The proving temperature should be at least 75°F. Try to be patient at this stage and let them expand as much as possible.

If the loaves are round, when you turn them on to the peel dust them with flour, or else keep the proving baskets generously floured so the loaves carry some of this into the oven. Give them one deep diagonal slash with a razor blade or a sharp serrated knife. Bake on the oven floor at about 425°F for approximately 15 minutes. Cool on racks.

The oven needs to be ready for the completion of the final proof, which in effect means raking it out and letting it soak when the loaves are moulded, at which point it should have a temperature of around 550–600°F. Place a thermometer in the oven and keep the door closed. Just before the final proof is over, sweep out the ashes and use the scuffle or mop to clean the floor, checking all nails and foreign objects have been removed that might otherwise embed themselves in the crust, to the detriment of teeth. Replace the thermometer and close the door, checking the temperature one last time before charging the oven with loaves. When the fire was actually lit will depend on how often the oven is used, but see my comments on running the oven, above.

If the oven is too hot, really too hot, yet the bread will brook no delay, it is possible to put lots of water through the door (stand back so hands and eyebrows are not scalded) to bring down the heat on the sole. You can also bake with the door open to mitigate the radiation from the ceiling as an emergency measure.

If the oven seems hot yet not impossible, then consider where to place the loaves. If you are baking a full load, you have little choice, but if there is room to manoeuvre, the loaves can be placed in the coolest (or warmest) part of the oven depending on circumstance. In general, but this will depend on fire-building, the front of the oven is cooler, and keep the loaves away from the side walls if you wish to avoid scorching them.

When placing the loaves in the oven, the crust will be crisper if they are not too close together, and their rising will not be affected by their neighbour. If the loaves are in tins, baking will be slower. The black sheet steel tins give the best crust. If tins are lined in serried ranks, the side crusts will be very pale, and cooking delayed.

It is wise to check on progress (for which a torch is useful) four or five minutes after the bake has begun. If you have miscalculated the temperature or conditions inside the oven, you can plan remedial action. For instance, once the loaves have set, you can move them away from a hot spot to some cooler zone so that they do not burn too much.

Loaves that are baked on the oven floor usually have thick adamantine crusts when they are taken out. The usual test of tapping the bottom to see if they ring hollow still works, but the sound and vibration of the loaf in the hand are not the same as they are with a thin-skinned object removed from the sterile conditions of a gas cooker. One check is by weight – they feel light. They will have lost about 8–10 per cent of their weight by evaporation of moisture. This will increase to 12 per cent during cooling.

BAKING PIZZAS

There are many excellent recipe books for pizzas and other hearthbreads such as focaccia which will be more instructive than I on fillings, flavours, and other imponderables. Sufficient here to say that the important fact, argued persuasively by Elizabeth David, is they should be simple and pungent, not dustbin vehicles for anything vaguely Italian in the refrigerator. I would stress the importance of fresh herbs to the real success of a pizza.

Most British pizzas are composed and cooked on a pan. Nothing is better than directly on the oven bottom. It needs a degree of facility with the peel, and an encumbrance-free working area, but time in trial and error is well spent. Pizzas cooked like this, and consumed on the spot, will be much more tender and toothsome than those cooked for longer on metal in an electric oven.

If the oven has been heated for any time, cooking is tremendously rapid. If it were heated to cook but one pizza for personal consumption, it would be a terrible (apparent) waste of fuel, so a pizza-party is the obvious answer; or the pizza is cooked as a prelude to a bread baking session.

The embers are left in the oven during cooking, and the door left open, for different reasons. The embers are commonly left in the pizza oven because the baker is using it for production all day, or at least all the meal, long. The oven, therefore will need refreshing, so the embers are stoked and revived to make a small fire to give more flash heat. The door is left open because pizzas and other hearthbreads were cooked at the beginning of a session, when the oven was at its hottest. A closed door was simply not necessary. It is of course not imperative that the embers are left in, or the door left open, to cook a matchless pizza in your own oven.

Figure 69: a medieval bakehouse, with a flaming brand in the mouth of the oven to pro-vide light. Two sizes of loaf are in preparation. The assistant is ready to pass the baker the next candidate for the peel, an action also shown in figure 7. The bread must have been sturdier, or less proved, than a loaf trembling for the oven today.

Figure 70: an eighteenth-century French baker's shop; a companion piece to figures 53 and 54. Bread is being sold by weight on the right; loaves are stacked well out of harm's, and dirt's, way on shelves in the upper reaches; a boy is ready to set off on deliveries, tal-lies dangling from his waistband; the girl on the left is chipping crusts with a knife.

BIBLIOGRAPHY

Eliza Acton, *The English Bread Book for Domestic Use*, London 1857 (reprinted, Lewes, 1990)

W.J. Ashley, *The Bread of our Forefathers*, Oxford 1928

Richard M. Bacon, *The Forgotten Art of Building and Using a Brick Bake Oven*, Dublin, New Hampshire 1977

Walter T. Banfield, *Manna*, London 1937

Peter Beacham, ed., *Devon Building*, Exeter 1990

Kerstin Bernhard, *bröd pain ψωμι*, Stockholm 1969

Lise Boily & Jean-François Blanchette, *The Bread Ovens of Quebec*, Ottawa 1979

Peter Brears, *The Gentlewoman's Kitchen, Great Food in Yorkshire* 1650–1750, Wakefield 1984

Peter Brears, *The Kitchen Catalogue*, York 1979

John Burnett, *Plenty & Want. A Social History of Diet in England from 1815 to the Present Day*, London 1966 [1979]

R. Calvel, *La boulangerie moderne*, Paris, 3rd edition 1962

The Cookery Book of Lady Clark of Tillypronie (1909), reprinted Lewes 1994

Anthony Cubberley, 'Bread-baking in Ancient Italy', *Food in Antiquity*, ed. Wilkins, Harvey & Dobson, Exeter 1995

Elizabeth David, *English Bread and Yeast Cookery*, London 1977

Alan Davidson, ed., *The Cook's Room*, London 1991

Caroline Davidson, *A woman's work is never done*, London 1982

Françoise Desportes, *Le pain au moyen âge*, Paris 1987

A. Edlin, *A Treatise on the Art of Bread-Making*, London 1805 (reprinted Prospect Books, 1992)

William Ellis, *The Country Housewife's Family Companion*, London and Salisbury 1750

Alexander Fenton, *Scottish Country Life*, Edinburgh 1976

Carol Field, *The Italian Baker*, New York 1985

Gillian Goodwin, *Manchet & Trencher*, London 1983

Alison Grant, *North Devon Pottery: The Seventeenth Century*, Exeter 1983

Todd Gray, ed., *Devon Household Accounts, 1627-59*, Devon & Cornwall Record Society, NS vol. 38, Exeter 1995

Ann Hagen, *A Handbook of Anglo-Saxon Food, Processing and Consumption*, Pinner 1992

H.P. Hansen, *Bondens Brød*, Copenhagen 1954

Dorothy Hartley, *Food in England*, London 1954

Marie Hartley & Joan Ingilby, *Life and Tradition in the Yorkshire Dales*, London 1968

M.A. Havinden, ed., *Household and Farm Inventories in Oxfordshire, 1550–1590*, London & Oxford 1965

John Holloway, ed., *The Oxford Book of Local Verses*, Oxford 1987

Houlston's Industrial Library, No. 1, *The Baker*, London n.d.

Tom Jaine, 'England: Castle Hill', in C. Anne Wilson, ed., *Traditional Country House Cooking*, London 1993

Tom Jaine, *Making Bread at Home*, London 1995

Maria Kaneva-Johnson, *The Melting Pot: Balkan Food and Cookery*, Totnes 1995

E.J. Kenney, ed., *The Ploughman's Lunch, Moretum*, Bristol 1984

John Kirkland, *The Modern Baker, Confectioner and Caterer*, London 1907

Alan Macfarlane, ed., *The Diary of Ralph Josselin 1616–1683*, London 1976

Michel Marin, *Construire, restaurer, utiliser les fours à pain*, Paris 1995

Edith Martin, comp., *Cornish Recipes Ancient and Modern*, Truro 1929

Stephen Mennell, 'Indigestion in the 19th Century, Aspects of English Taste and Anxiety', in *Taste. Proceedings of the Oxford Symposium 1987*, London 1988

W.S. Merwin, 'Shepherds', *Paris Review* 101, 1986

The New Female Instructor; or, Young Woman's Guide to Domestic Happiness, published by Thomas Kelly, London c.1833

Joe Ortiz, *The Village Baker*, Berkeley, California 1993

J.H. Parker, *Some Account of Domestic Architecture in England, from Richard II to Henry VIII*, Oxford 1859

Parmentier, A.A., *Le Parfait Boulanger, ou Traité Complet Sur la Fabrication & le Commerce du Pain*, Paris 1778 (reprinted Marseille, 1981)

Lionel Poilâne, *Guide de l'amateur de pain*, Paris 1981

D. Portman, *Exeter Houses 1400–1700*, Exeter 1966

Eileen Power, trans., *The Goodman of Paris*, London 1928 [1992]

Jaakko Rahola, 'Bread Shapes in Finland', *Look and Feel. Proceedings of the Oxford Symposium 1993*, Totnes 1994

Barbara Santich, 'Testo, Tegamo, Tiella, Tian: the Mediterranean Camp Oven', *The Cooking Pot. Proceedings of the Oxford Symposium on Food and Cookery 1988* , London 1989

Terence Scully, *The Art of Cookery in the Middle Ages*, Woodbridge, 1995

Ronald Sheppard & Edward Newton, *The Story of Bread*, London 1937

Janet Shirley, trans., *A Parisian Journal 1405–1449*, Oxford 1968

Nancy Silverton, 'A Lesson in Baking Bread', *Gourmet*, March 1996

Louis Stouff, *Ravitaillement et alimentation en Provence aux XIV*^{e} *et XV*^{e} *siècles*, Paris 1970

Sylvia Thrupp, *A Short History of the Worshipful Company of Bakers of London*, London 1933

Joyce Tyldesley, *Daughters of Isis*, London 1994

Unione Tipografico-Editrice Torinese, *Gastronomia del Rinascimento a cura di Luigi Firpo, Turin 1974* (for illustrations from Bartolomeo Scappi)

Eveline J. van der Steen, 'Fiery Furnaces: bread ovens in the ancient Near East', *Petits Propos Culinaires* 42, 1992

Margaret M. Verney, *Memoirs of the Verney Family*, London 1892 [1970]

Rosemary Weinstein, 'Kitchen Chattels: the Evolution of Familiar Objects 1200–1700', *The Cooking Pot. Proceedings of the Oxford Symposium 1988*, London 1989

Thomas White, *A Treatise on the Art of Baking*, Edinburgh 1828

C.M. Woolgar, ed., *Household Accounts from Medieval England*, Records of Social and Economic History, NS vols. XVII & XVIII, London 1992

Doreen Yarwood, *The British Kitchen*, London 1981

NOTES AND MEMORANDA

NOTES AND MEMORANDA

NOTES AND MEMORANDA

NOTES AND MEMORANDA

NOTES AND MEMORANDA

NOTES AND MEMORANDA

NOTES AND MEMORANDA